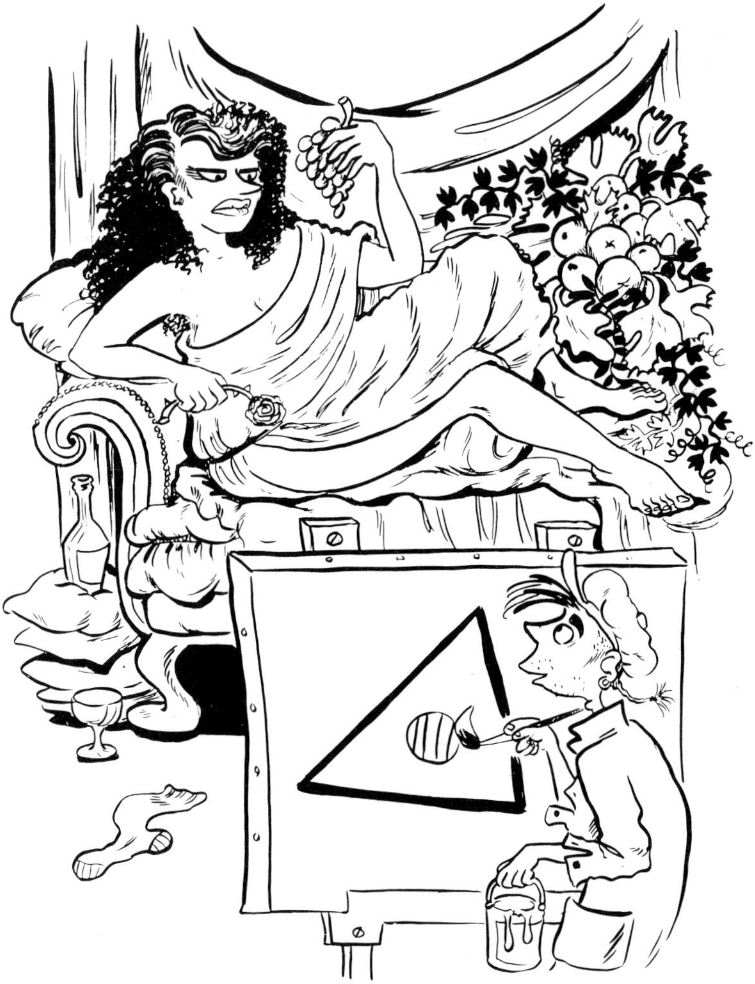

GRAPHIC GUIDES

Series editor: Philip Boys

Anarchy

Clifford Harper

Animal Liberation

Lori Gruen, Peter Singer & David Hine

Apartheid

Donald Woods & Mike Bostock

Media and Power

Peter Lewis & Corinne Pearlman

Modern Art

Dave Clarke & Julie Hollings

Space Wars

Martin Ince & David Hine

Thatcher

Ed Harriman & John Freeman

Women Artists

Frances Borzello & Natacha Ledwidge

Forthcoming titles

The Birth of the Woman's Novel

Dale Spender & Natacha Ledwidge

Language and Power

Rob Pope & Graham Higgins

Logic and Power

Herb Kohl & Robin Collingwood

Revolutionary Women

Cathy Porter & Anna Louise

Radiation and Health

Tony Webb & Robin Collingwood

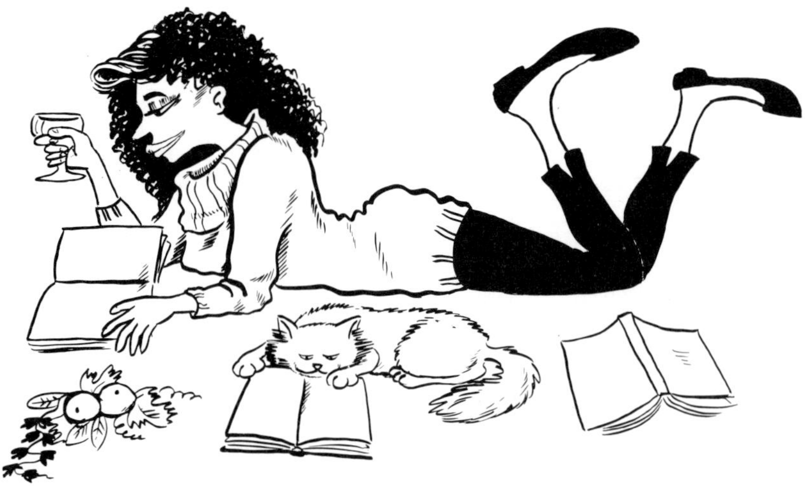

MODERN ART
a graphic guide

Text: David Clarke
Illustrations: Julie Hollings

Camden Press

Published in 1987 by
Camden Press Ltd
43 Camden Passage, London N1 8EB England

Designed by Julie Hollings & Terry Howe

Set in 12 on 14pt Optima Roman by Character Typesetting London EC1 and printed and bound in Great Britain by Richard Clay Ltd (The Chaucer Press), Suffolk

British Library Cataloguing in Publication Data
Clarke, Dave, Modern Art: a graphic guide. —
(Graphic guides)

1. Art, Modern — 19th century

2. Art, Modern — 20th century

I. Title II. Hollings, Julie III. Series 709'.04 N6447

ISBN 0-948491-18-3

To my mother and my brother and in memory of my father.

Thanks are due to Frances and Bob Borzello for the support and encouragement they gave this project from its earliest stages, and to Philip Boys for his painstaking and sympathetic editing.
(Dave Clarke)

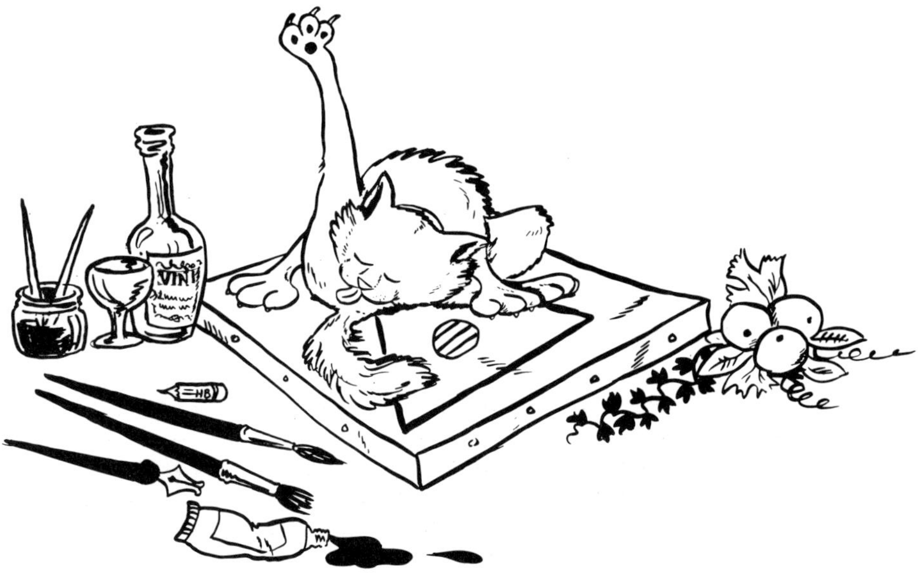

VIN
HB

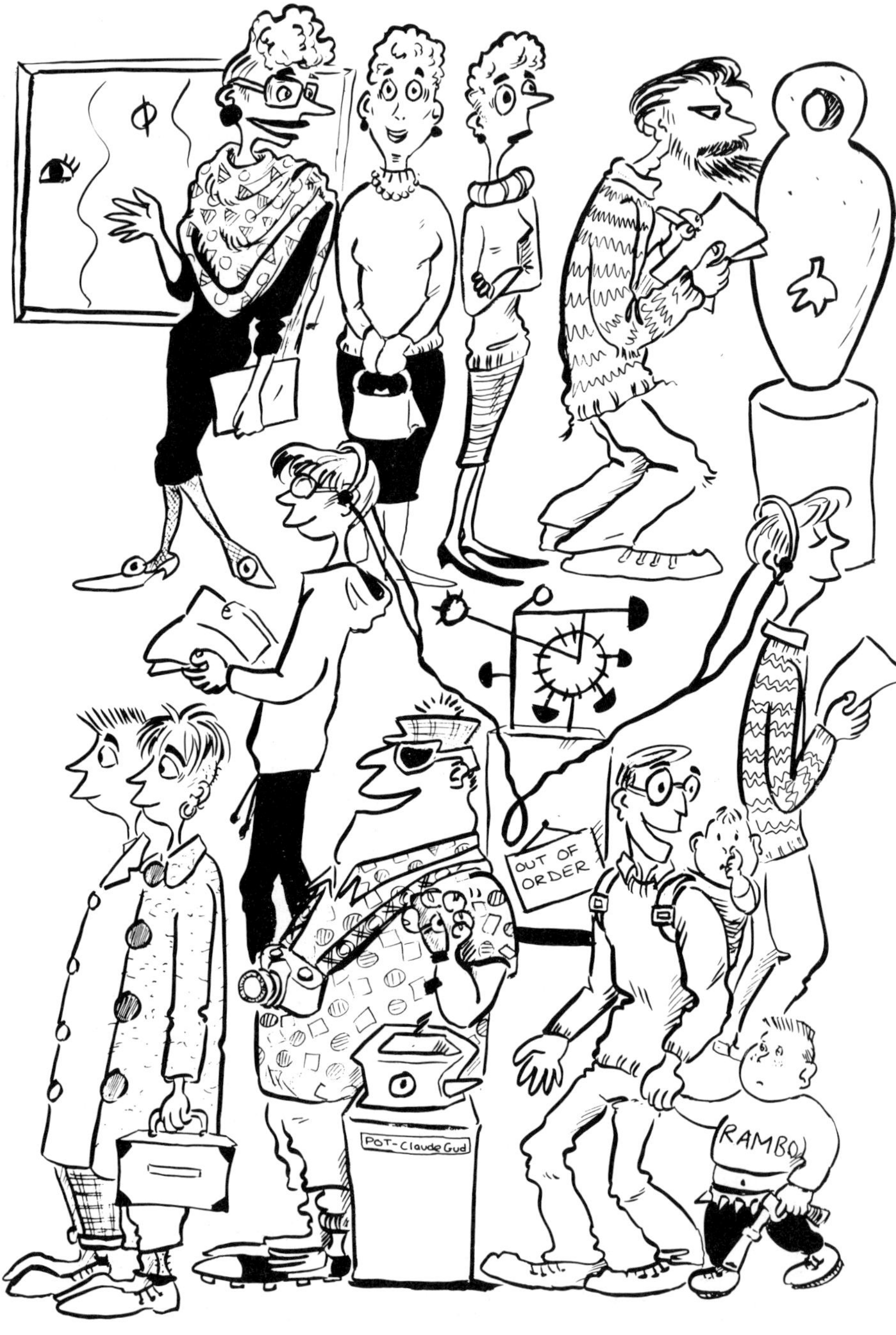
OUT OF ORDER
POT-Claude Gud
RAMBO

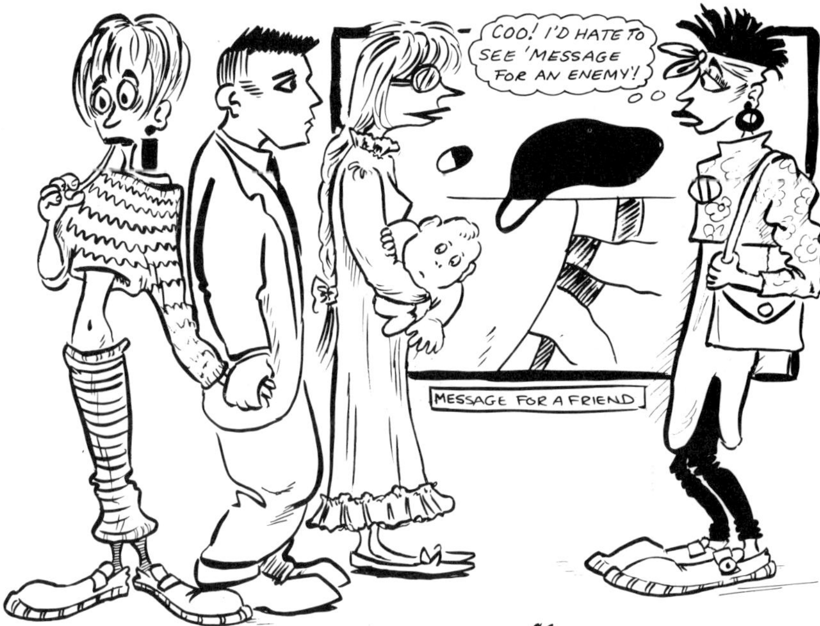
COO! I'D HATE TO SEE 'MESSAGE FOR AN ENEMY'!
MESSAGE FOR A FRIEND

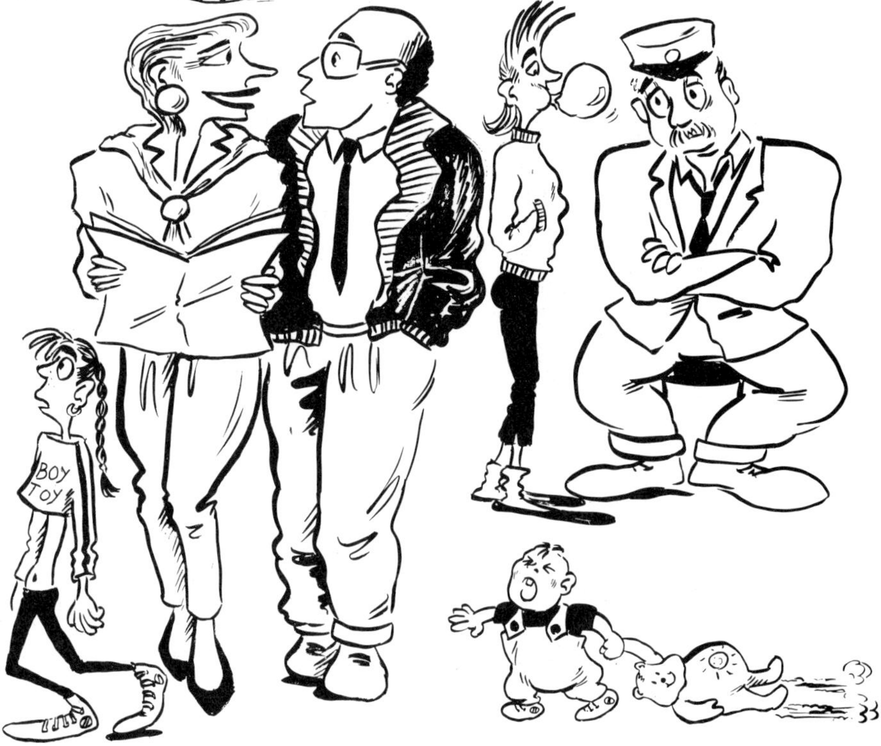
BOY TOY

Form

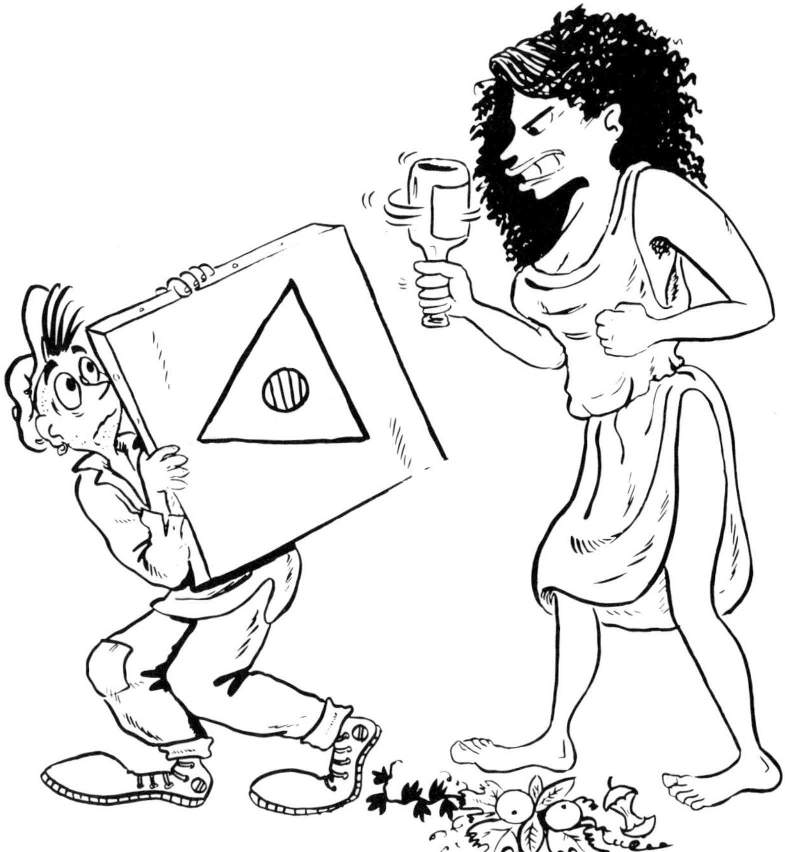

Of all the criticisms that are made of modern art, perhaps the most common is the one which dismisses it as *not realistic enough*. This complaint can be phrased in different ways, but it boils down to a belief that art is better the closer it is to life — the more 'photographic' it gets. Modern artists are dismissed as at best lacking in skill, at worst as being confidence tricksters.

This book won't be giving such a belief its stamp of approval. Throughout its pages we'll be seeing the limitations of using this standard of 'lifelikeness' (more appropriate to the waxworks museum than the art gallery) to judge modern art by . . . or indeed any art. *Absolute realism in art is not possible,* even if it were desirable.

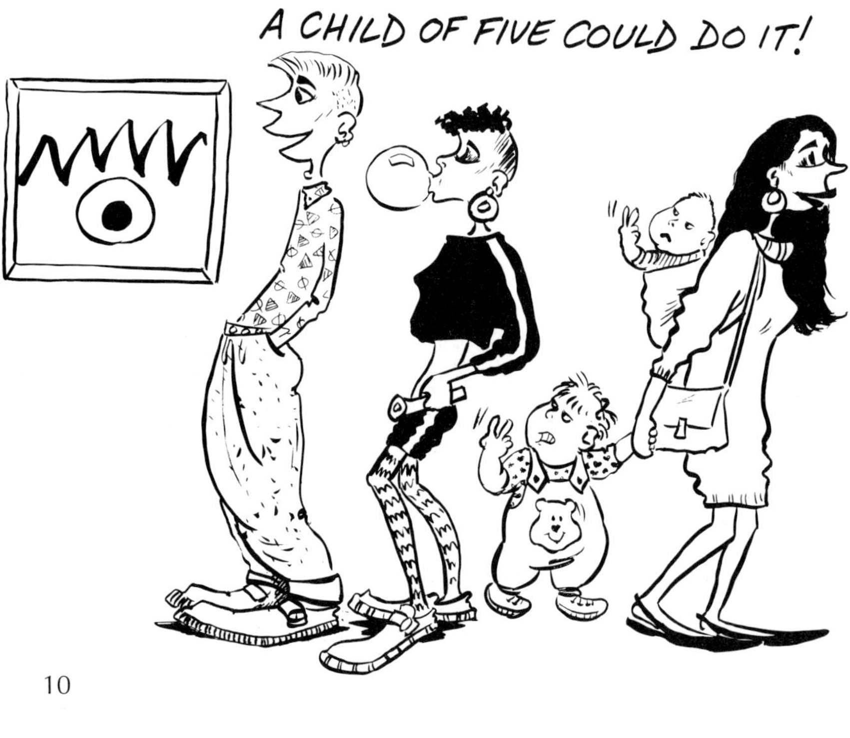

Those who prefer 'realistic' art to modern styles often use the words 'photographic' to describe work they approve of, as if a photo were a pure likeness of its subject, providing an objective standard against which paintings can be judged. Yet even here this notion of 'realism' is inadequate. The image the camera produces is affected by many factors other than the subject itself — the type of lens and film used, the length of exposure, the developing time, and so on.

For instance, the choice of exposure time affects how much light there is in the photograph. It's not a question of how much illumination there is at any one time in the scene being shot, but the total amount of light that gets onto the film. A long exposure can make even a very dark scene appear much lighter, and vice versa. A short exposure can also freeze a very rapid motion, such as that of an insect's wing during flight. Is such a photo 'realistic', even though it produces an image that the naked eye could never see?

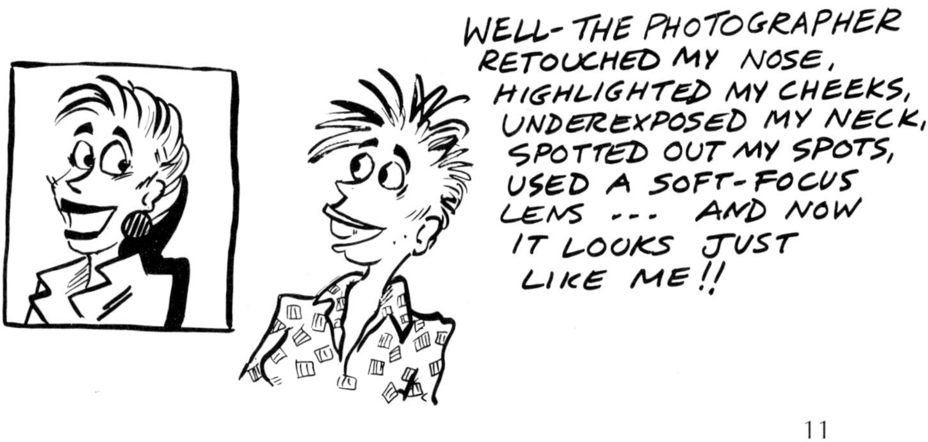

We find even more difficulties with the idea of 'realism' when we start to apply it to paintings. How is an artist 'realistically' to reproduce, say, sunlight? There is no pigment on the palette which actually emits light as the sun does; paint merely reflects it. So how ever hard an artist tries, the luminosity of a sunny scene cannot be captured. As Paul Cézanne, one of the pioneers of modern art, put it:

'I wished to copy nature. I could not. But I was satisfied when I discovered that the sun, for instance, could not be reproduced, but that it must be represented by something else . . . by colour.'

Cézanne realized that there was an essential difference between 'art' and 'life'. Sunlight could only be rendered in art by creating an equivalent — by coloured paint. Like other modern artists he saw this gap between the painted world and the real world not as a limitation for art, but as giving it a greater freedom in deciding how to present life. Rather than be judged by the standards of nature, art must follow its own rules.

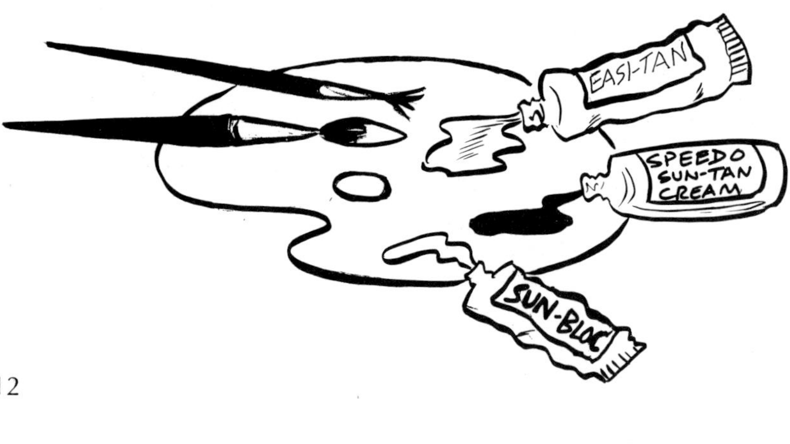

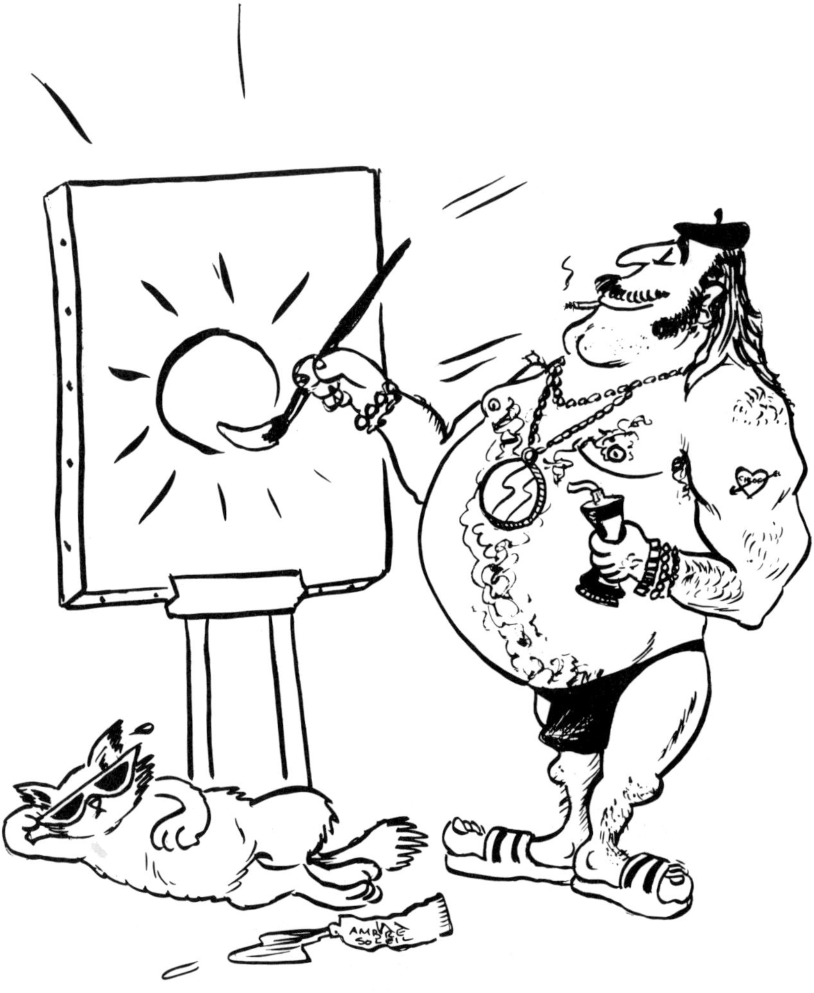
AMBRE SOLEIL

Before the modern era, painting was often *illusionistic*. That is to say, it tried to trick the spectator's eye into believing that rather than containing a flat canvas, the frame was like a window opening onto another world as real as the one in which the viewer stood. Such an illusion could never be complete for the spectator, but it added to the confusion between art and life.

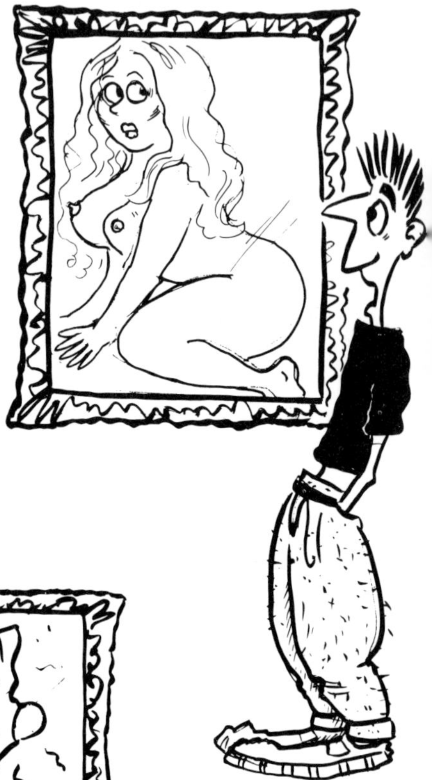

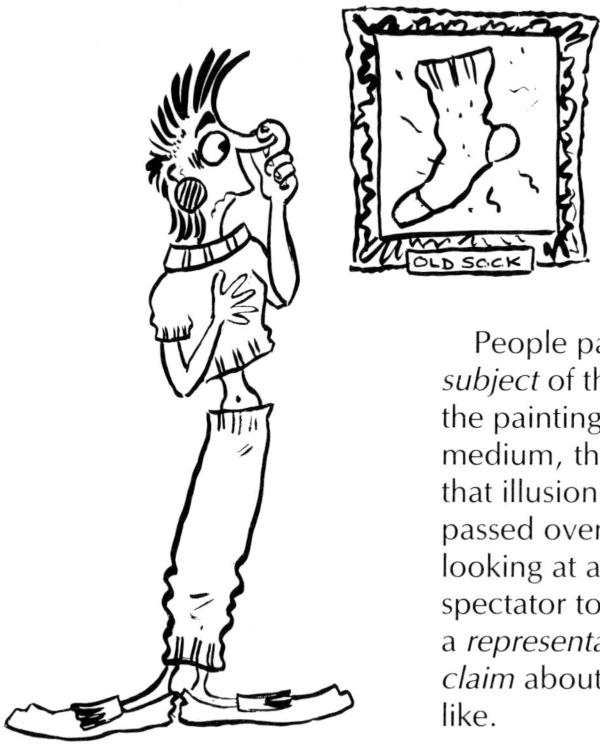

People paid attention to the *subject* of the painting, not to the painting itself. The medium, the means by which that illusion was created, was passed over. This way of looking at art has blinded the spectator to the fact that art is a *representation* of reality — a *claim* about what reality is like.

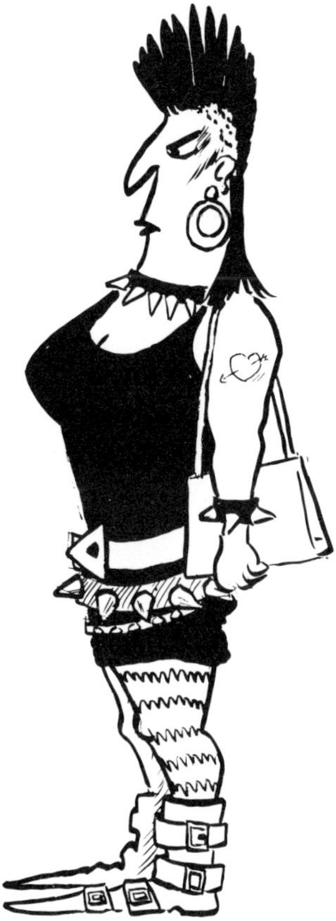

A painting does not innocently mirror life; it is a constructed image, made by a human hand out of particular materials with qualities of their own.

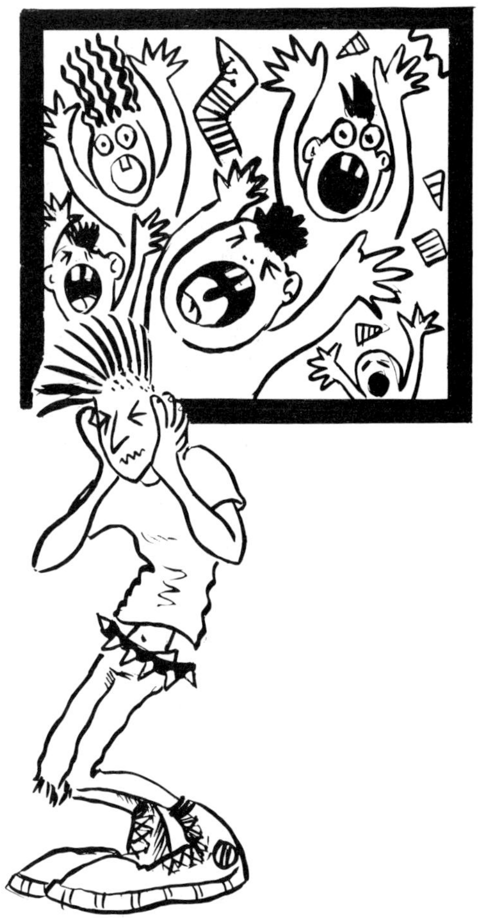

All art involves a process of selection: the artist has to make a series of choices about which aspects of the subject to allow into the painting and which to exclude. The richness of reality cannot all be squashed onto a flat surface, even in the most detailed painting.

Neither is the outcome inevitable: the painting could have evolved in many different ways. Even the most 'realistic' of artists will paint the same scene differently from one another, and not just for 'aesthetic' reasons.

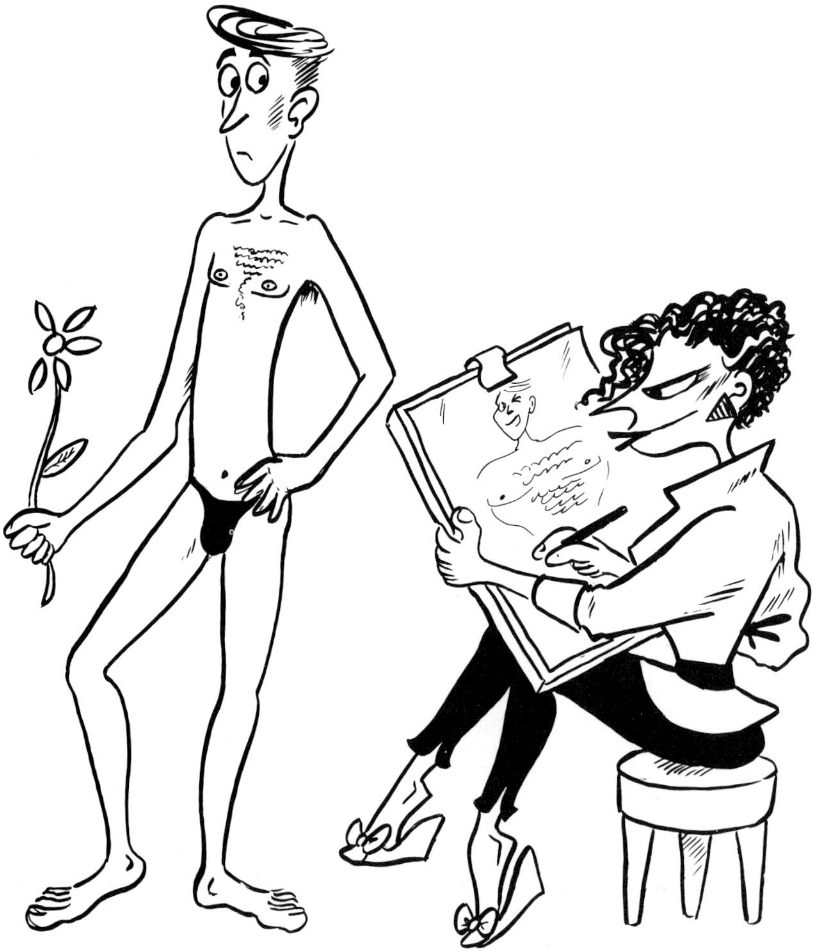

Decisions made in the painting process will be conditioned — explicitly or implicitly — by extra-artistic experience and beliefs.

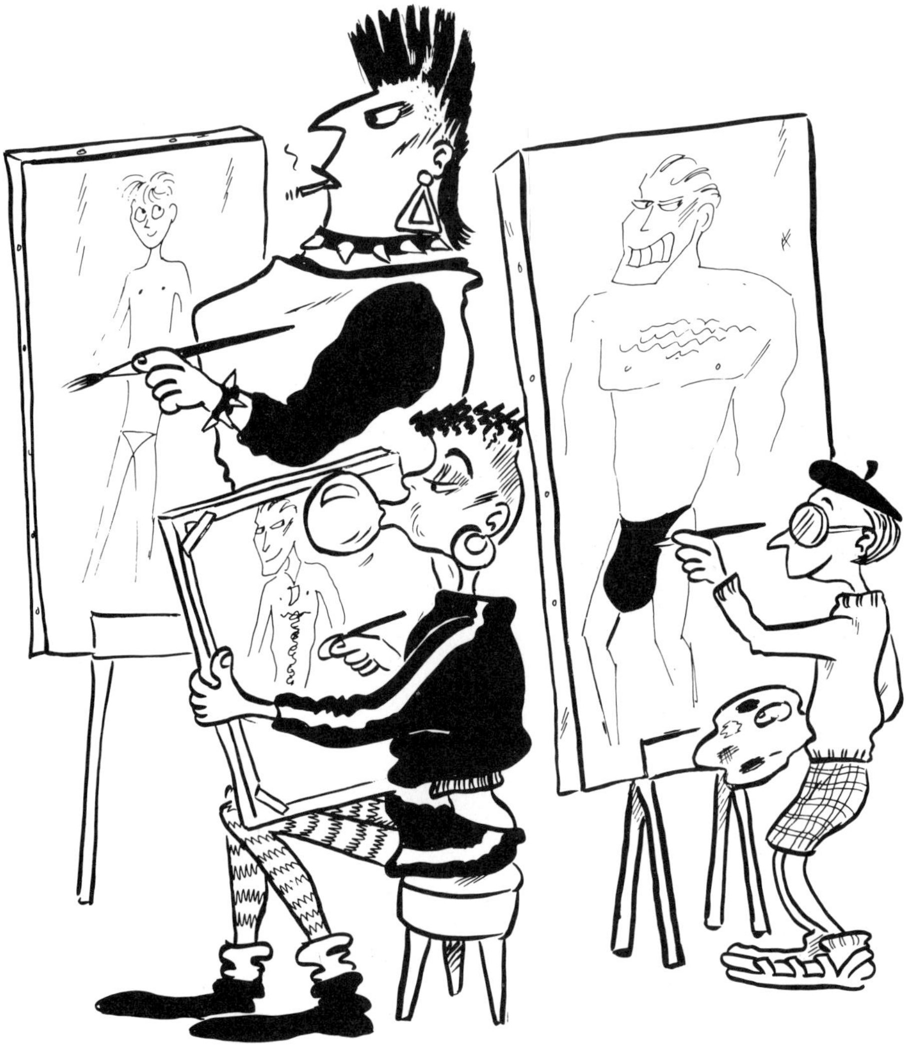

Maybe it seems obvious that — to put it at its crudest — reality is three-dimensional (and alive) whereas a painting is flat (and static), but it's easily overlooked all the same. The confusion between art and life — the tendency to 'mistake the map for the territory' — runs very deep.

For instance, to most people's eyes a precise outline drawing would seem essentially more realistic than a Cubist work like Pablo Picasso's *Seated Nude* of 1909-10.

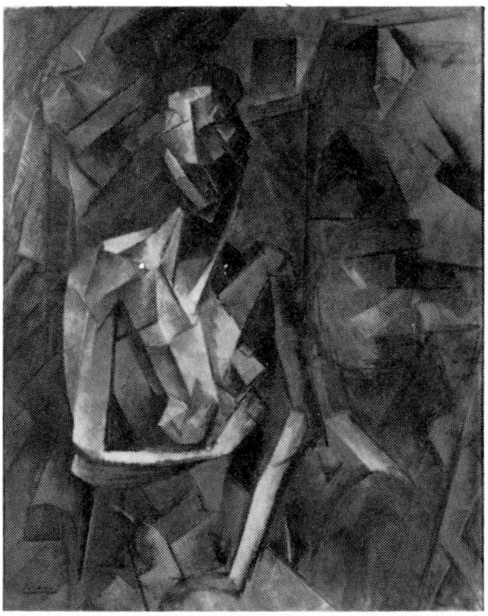

Pablo Picasso *Seated Nude* 1909-10

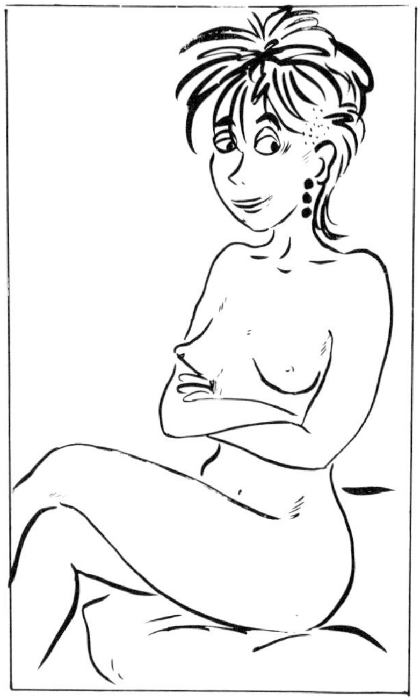

It takes, perhaps, a step outside our preconceptions to see that a human head is no more made up grey lines than it is made up of angular planes. A line is something essentially abstract and artificial, something never met within the real world, and which is used in drawings to symbolize the separateness of the sitter from her background.

Consider the issue the other way round. Suppose some visitors from another planet were to discover a piece of paper with this design on it:

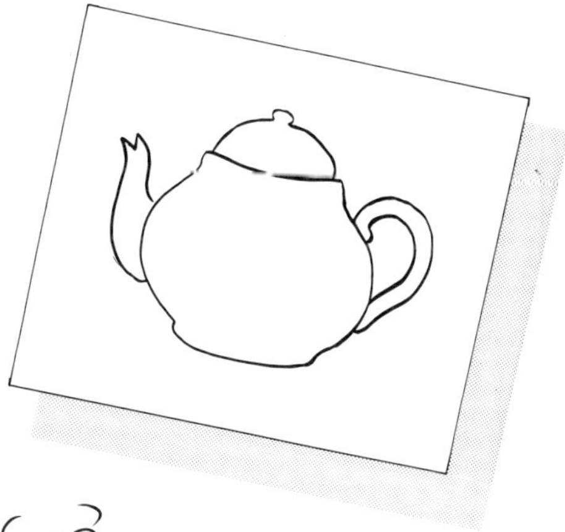

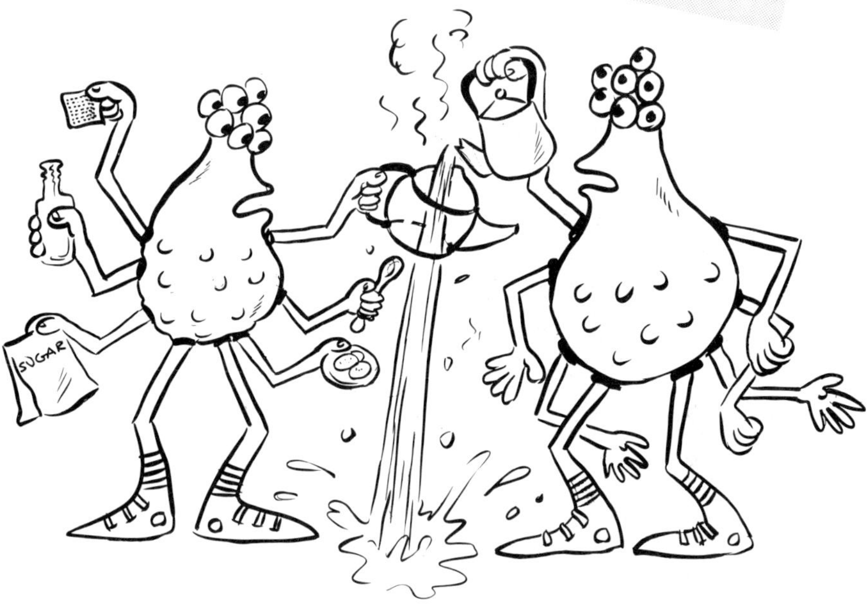

What if they tried to make the object depicted; what are the odds that they'd actually come up with a teapot? Might they not try to construct an object represented by the black lines as if those lines were all there was to the object? Would they know that the white space within the boundary line was a part of the object, unlike the white space outside it?

Art, then, is governed by codes or conventions which belong to it alone. All art is conventional — there is no 'styleless style', no 'natural' work of art — but the conventions of our own time and culture have a tendency to become invisible to us. They seem to have a 'natural rightness' simply because of our familiarity with them.

Modern art can look strange not so much because it's more conventionalized — more stylized — but just because the codes it uses are alien, so we notice them immediately.

When we call a picture 'realistic' we're perhaps not commenting on how much information about the world it contains, or how accurate this information is in some absolute sense, but in fact making a statement about the ease with which we can 'read' or decode it. Clearly this is a relative matter, dependent for instance on the nature and extent of our personal education and on the degree of social dominance a particular artistic code has attained.

Auguste Rodin, who could be called the first modern sculptor, sometimes created works (such as *Walking Man* of 1877-8) which featured fragmented human figures.

These works were very influential on later modern sculpture, but *Walking Man* was criticized at the time for its incompleteness, for its lack of a head and arms. Part of Rodin's defence was to point out that for thousands of years sculptured portrait busts had been popular, and no one had criticized *them* for being 'fragmentary'.

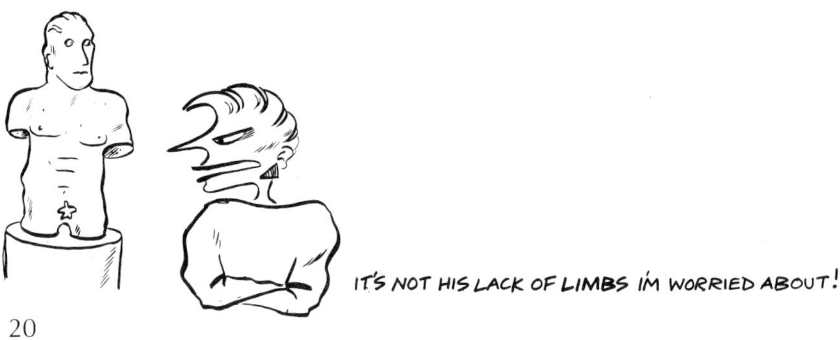

Familiarity can make even very 'unrealistic' conventions seem quite natural. It never seems strange, for instance, when people in operas or musicals sing rather than talk to each other.

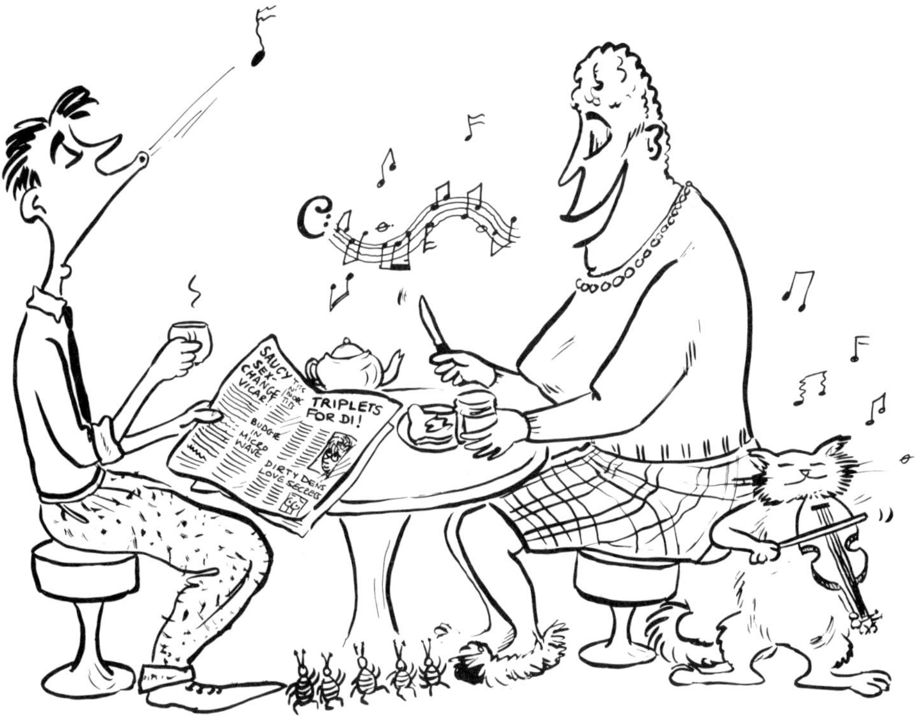

And how often do we ask ourselves why foreigners in British or American films generally talk among themselves in fluent English?

Or how come when screen lovers finally make it to the clinch we are there too, two inches away from their lips?

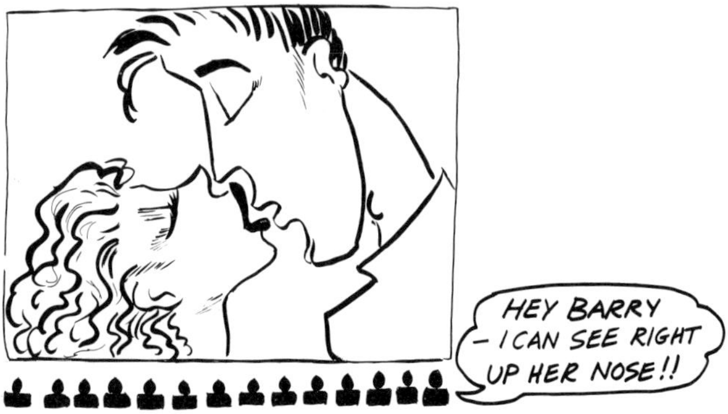

Likewise, when travelling to other countries: the manners and dress often seem strange (especially at first), whereas the complex rules that govern our own behaviour remain unquestioned, as if ours were the only correct way of going about things.

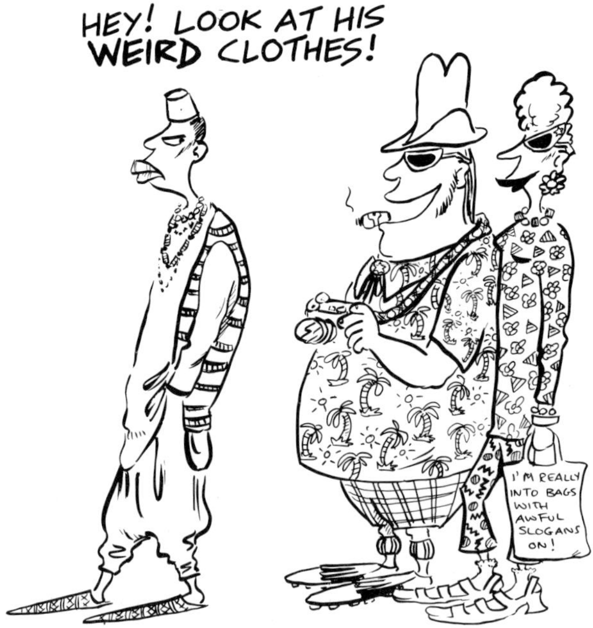

Many modern artists, becoming aware of the distinction we're discussing here between art and the world to which it refers, have felt they should give more of their attention than previous artists had done to the painting as an object in its own right. For them a painting does not merely re-present other things but is a thing in itself. This is seen as something to acknowledge openly, indeed to draw attention to.

The extreme case of this outlook is summed up in the expression 'Art for Art's sake', a phrase which became popular at the end of the 19th century to denote a concern with 'pure painting' — with producing an image pleasing in design terms alone. But while artists have generally become less interested in using paint to produce a resemblance of something or to tell some kind of story (say, from history or mythology), they have not generally lost interest in content. They just don't want content emphasized at the expense of the spectator's awareness of the intrinsic, literal qualities of painting. Here is how the artist and critic Maurice Denis, writing in 1890, expressed this shift of priorities:

'It is well to remember that a picture — before being a battle horse, a nude woman, or some anecdote — is essentially a flat surface covered with colours arranged in a certain order.'

An important way in which modern artists have emphasized painting's separateness from life has been by drawing attention to the *flatness* of the canvas surface. They have done this chiefly through abandoning shading — the use of light and dark tones to given an illusion of three-dimensional form — and by breaking with the rules of perspective.

Take, for example, Henri Matisse's *Open Window, Collioure* of 1905. Our first impression is of a decorative pattern on a two-dimensional surface. Although we can still read a sense of depth in the image, we also see the forms of the boats at anchor as if they lay on the same plane as the potted plants. Interior and exterior space seems continuous; we don't have the feeling that the painting has a hole in it. Matisse is perhaps the most important colourist in twentieth-century painting, but in this black and white reproduction we can see more clearly than in the original that he has not used light and dark to model depth.

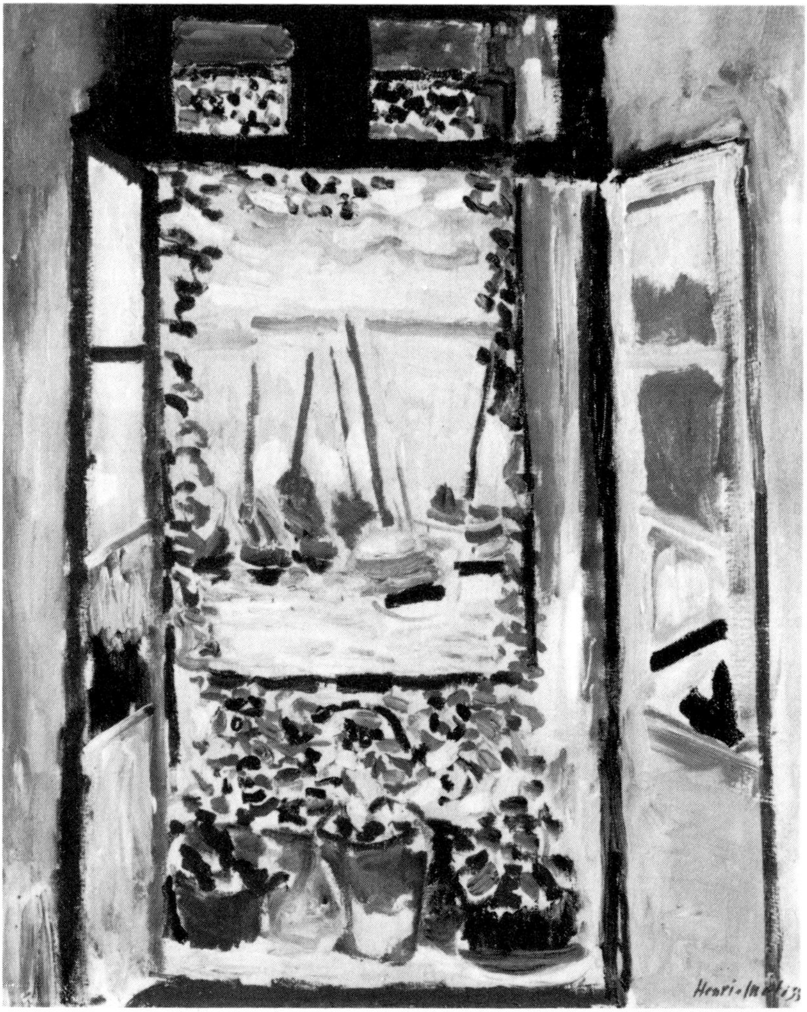

Henri Matisse *Open Window, Collioure* 1905

At first sight modern paintings which break the rules of perspective may 'feel wrong'. Yet perspective is a good example of an artistic convention which, because we are so used to it, seems not to be a convention at all but part of the way things really are. It appears to have scientific or mathematical authority.

In fact, of course, many other cultures manage to represent space in a painting quite adequately without our system for constructing a unified spatial illusion.
In a Persian miniature, for instance, the artist shows us that one figure is behind another by placing him or her higher up the page. One person can be larger than another in some pre-Renaissance conventions of painting, not to convey the information that they're nearer, but to inform the viewer that they're more important.

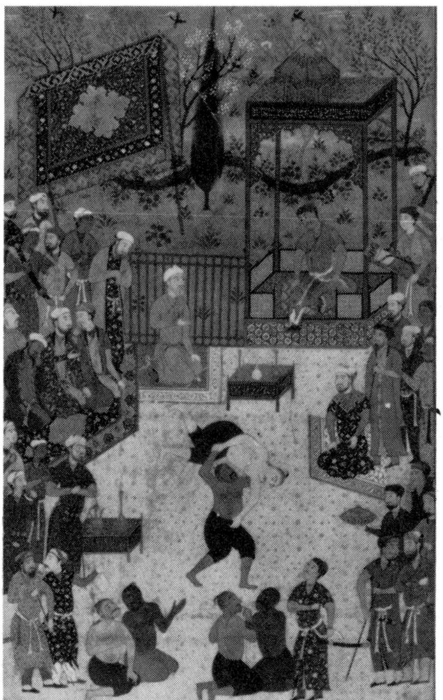

A Wrestling Match in Ancient Persia early 17th century

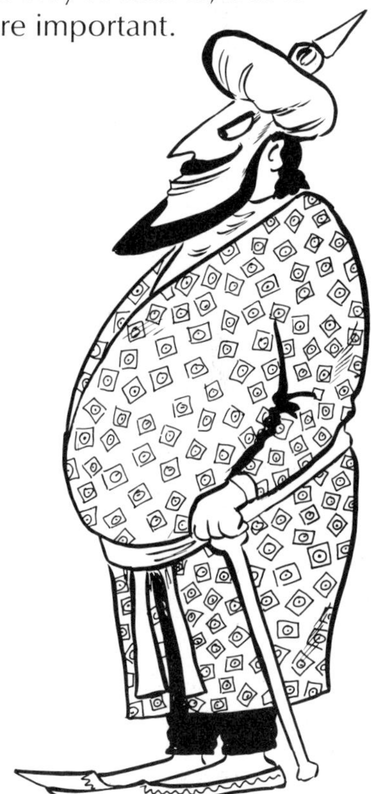

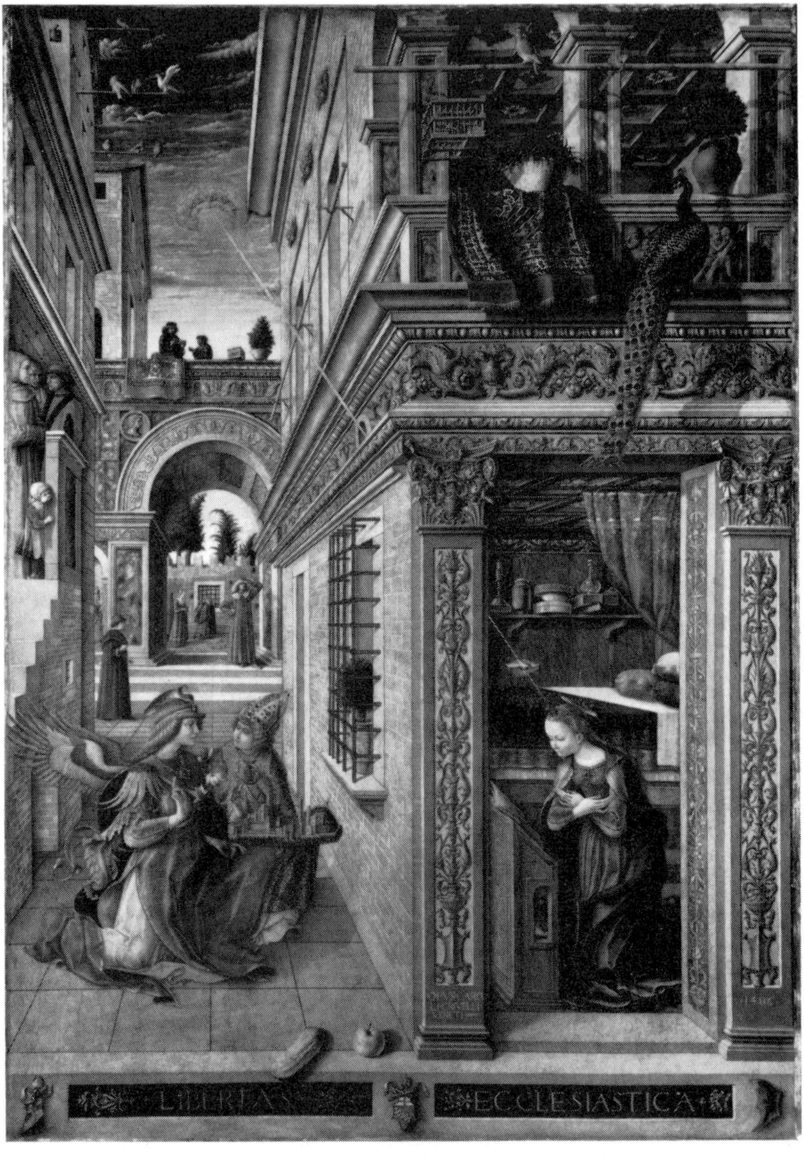

Carlo Crivelli *The Annunciation with St Emidius* 1486

The spatial illusion of Renaissance perspective makes sense in a painting only if we are standing with our eye at the level of the horizon and directly in front of the vanishing point. From any other viewpoint, it won't 'read' correctly. The artificiality of this convention should be obvious. For a start, we see the world not from one but two viewpoints — our two eyes. And in any case we rarely view from a static position. To take in a scene we tend to scan, adopting differing viewpoints for different objects.

It could even be argued that Cubist paintings (such as Pablo Picasso's *Seated Nude* of 1909) are closer to how we actually perceive things than a Renaissance image is able to be. The fragmentation of these images, which gives them their distinctive 'Cubist' look, is the result of the artist adding together information from more than one viewpoint.

A further tactic which modern artists have used to shift the viewer's attention to the work of art as object in its own right has been to emphasize the materials they have used.

The choice of materials always affects the kind of image that can be made; technique always influences style. (Think of the difference between an oil painting, a drawing and a mosaic of the same subject). However, in the oil paintings of the traditional 'academic' masters (whose work the moderns were reacting against) the brushmarks tended to be carefully smoothed together — the paintings were highly 'finished'.

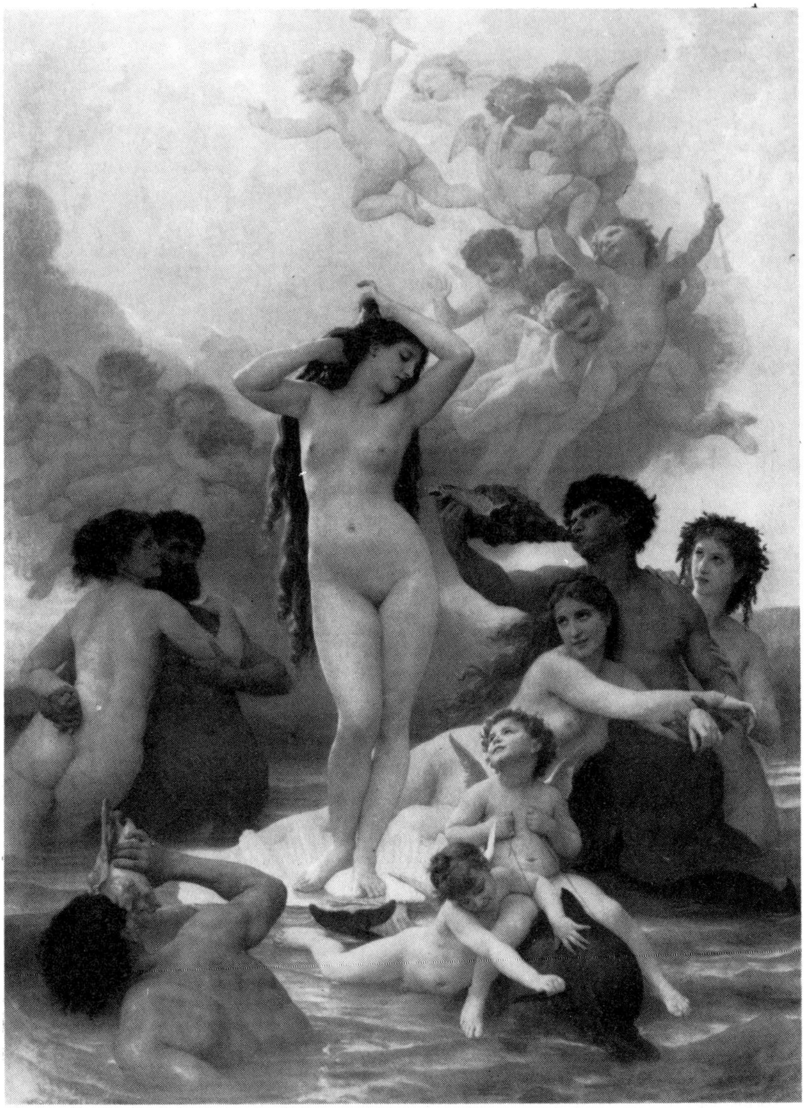

Adolphe Bouguereau *Birth of Venus* 1879

From the time of the Impressionists onwards, and with artists like Vincent Van Gogh and Matisse continuing the tendency, a more 'broken' quality of brushwork appears, a lack of 'finish'. One of the reasons for this shift was a desire amongst artists to emphasize to the viewer that paintings are made out of *paint*; they wanted to display the artificiality of art and its languages.

In *Open Window, Collioure,* we can distinguish the individual brushstrokes out of which the image has been created. The means of painting have become part of the subject of the painting itself. Picasso's *Seated Nude* is clearly made out of painted planes, not from flesh and blood, and Henry Moore's carvings (to give a sculptural example) openly exhibit the qualities of the stone or wood from which they are made.

Look, for instance, at his *Reclining Figure,* where the veining of the stone is clearly visible. We are made as

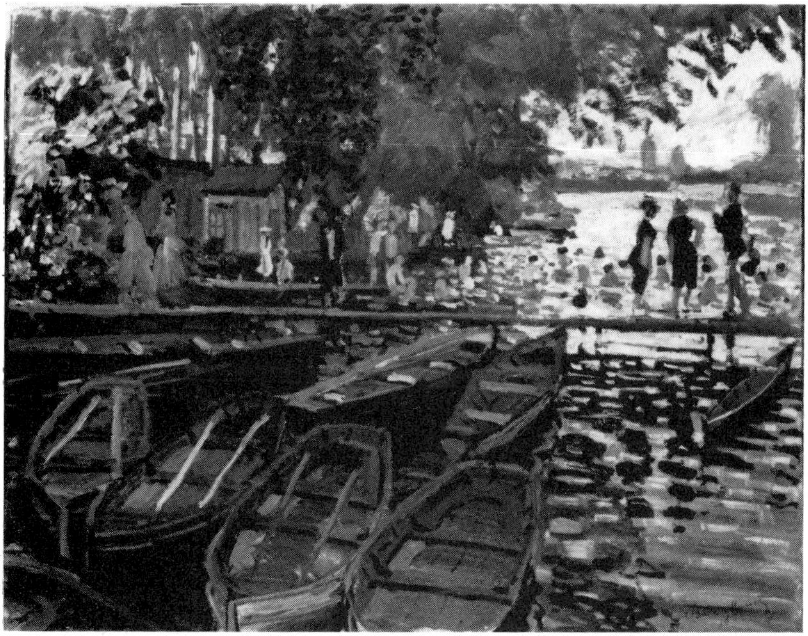

Claude Monet *Bathers at la Grenouillère* 1869

much aware of a form in stone as of a naked female body.

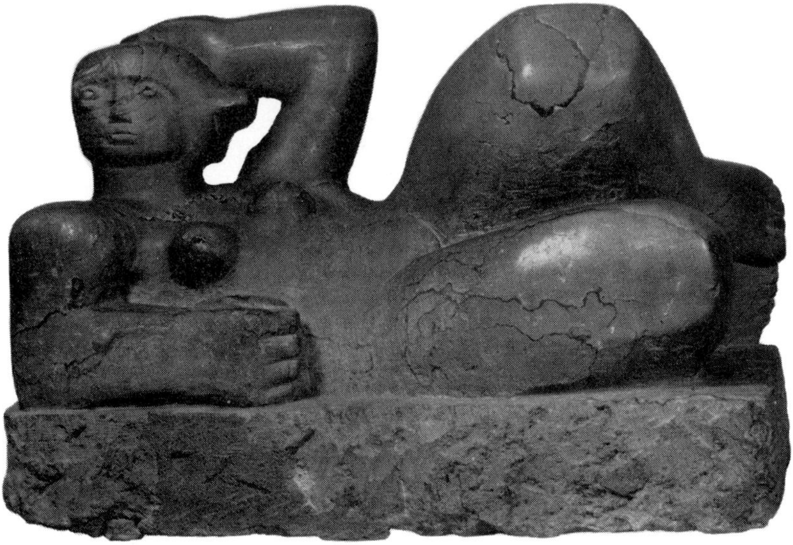

Henry Moore *Reclining Figure* 1929

Visible brushwork not only reveals to the spectator the nature of the materials being used, but also (by showing the traces of the artist's presence) makes it evident that the work is the product of a human hand and mind. Rather than a painting seeming to have come into being all of an instant — of its own accord, as it were — we have a sense of its production over time by a human agency.

In Rodin's *Kiss* of 1901-4, part of the block is left uncarved. Not only does this draw attention to the literal 'stoniness' of the sculpture, it also lets us see the artist's method of working. The creative process itself becomes part of the work's subject matter.

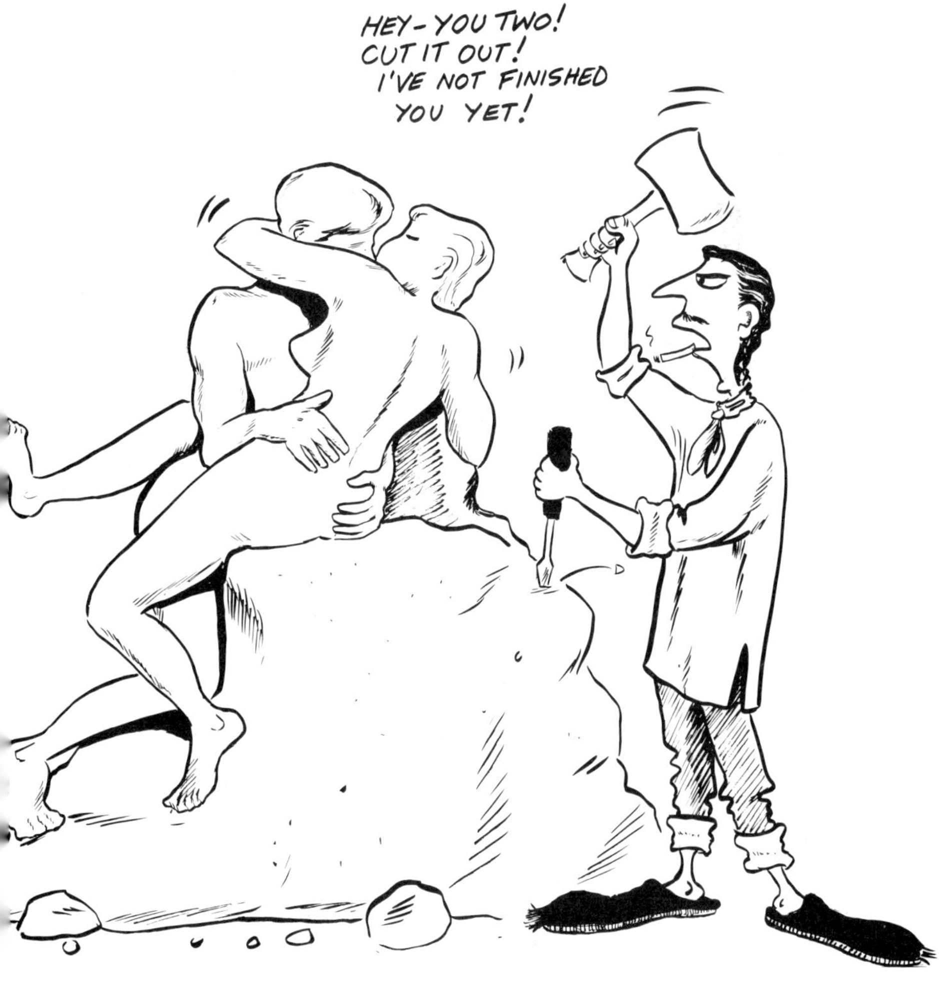

One of the basic qualities we look for in art is a harmony, a creation of order out of chaos. This is not just true of art — in life as well there is a fundamental human need for pattern or wholeness.

This search for unity is there in all art really, but modern artists are usually more willing to lay bare their compositional structures, to show how the artist's mind has created an ordered image out of inert materials, distorting natural forms so as to adjust them to the requirements of artistic pattern-making. Once resemblance to reality was abandoned as a criterion, art tended to be assessed more in accordance with its own standards: by the integration of its visual elements.

The concept of 'harmony' in art is difficult to define. We can make an analogy with music, although there the word has a more precise meaning. The rhyme and rhythm of poetry provide useful parallels because in their case (as in art's) distortions can occur in order to create a unity at the level of form. Poets and song-writers may force a rhyme, or stress a word in an unusual way to establish structure.

An instance of what we are discussing is Cézanne's *Still Life with Fruitbowl* of 1878. The 'knitted', directional quality of the brushstrokes is the means by which the artist has imposed a structural wholeness on the image. Similarly, the shapes in this painting are not selected (or their arrangement determined) solely by a desire for closeness to nature; they are tailored (or edited) for the role they play in the construction of a composed image.

For instance:

- ☐ The angle of the knife is designed to echo the angle of the cloth's left edge.
- ☐ The grapes hanging over the edge of the fruitbowl serve visually to 'break' the otherwise dominant line of the bowl's rim.
- ☐ The shape of the fruitbowl seems to have been elongated to create a necessary horizontal accent in the image, reinforcing the one established by the chest on which the still life is resting.
- ☐ We have a different viewpoint on the rim of the wineglass from the one we have on the surface of the liquid within it. This distortion creates shapes that 'rhyme' with those of the leaves on the wallpaper behind.

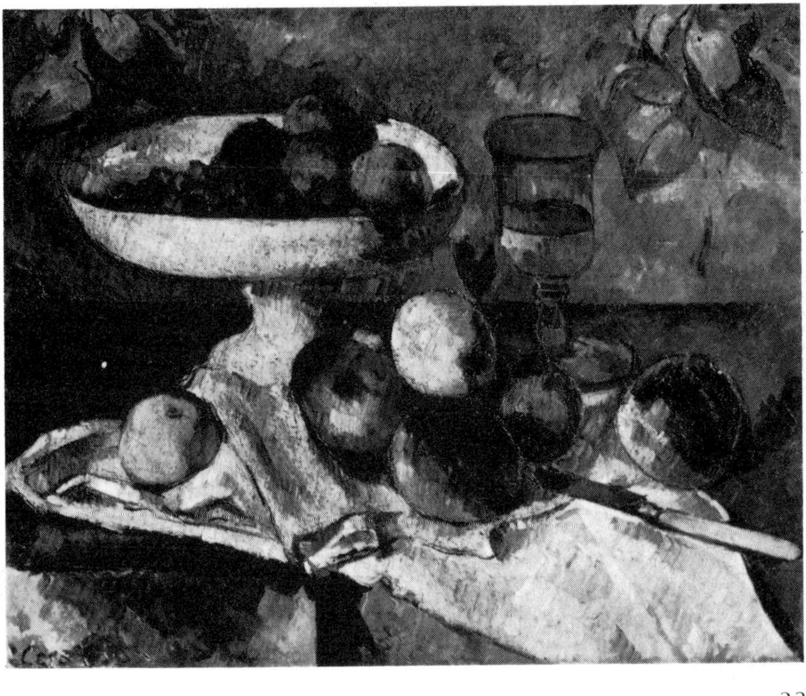

Paul Cézanne *Still Life with Fruitbowl* 1878

In Picasso's *Seated Nude* the same angular vocabulary of shapes is employed over the entire surface, and this helps produce a compositional unity. The subject and its surroundings are further linked into a whole by their shared colouring and by the establishment of 'visual rhymes' between fore- and background forms. This goal is achieved in an even more radical way in later Cubist works. The external boundaries of objects are fragmented, thus counteracting on a formal level the distinctions which the subject matter imposes.

The continuities created over the surface of the image help bring foreground and depth together, to re-establish the 'integrity' of the flat surface of the painting (another aspect of pictorial unity important for modern artists, as we've already mentioned). The shading of the planes in this and other Cubist works does give a sense of (shallow) depth but the shading is contradictory. The result is that the hints of depth cancel each other out, and our eye is 'returned' to the flatness of the canvas surface, to the sense of a two-dimensional design.

That desire to evoke both a sense of the third dimension and yet also to make a pleasing two-dimensional pattern is also present in Cézanne's painting. The tilted angle at which we view the lid of the chest helps flatten out the design emphasizing the canvas plane.

Matisse's *The Moroccans,* of 1916, is an even more pared down, abstracted work than either the Cézanne or the Picasso we have been examining. Modern artists, Matisse among them, have discovered and exploited the fact that detailed description is not necessary in order to evoke references to reality in art. Abbreviated signs are sufficient; cues alone can do the job.

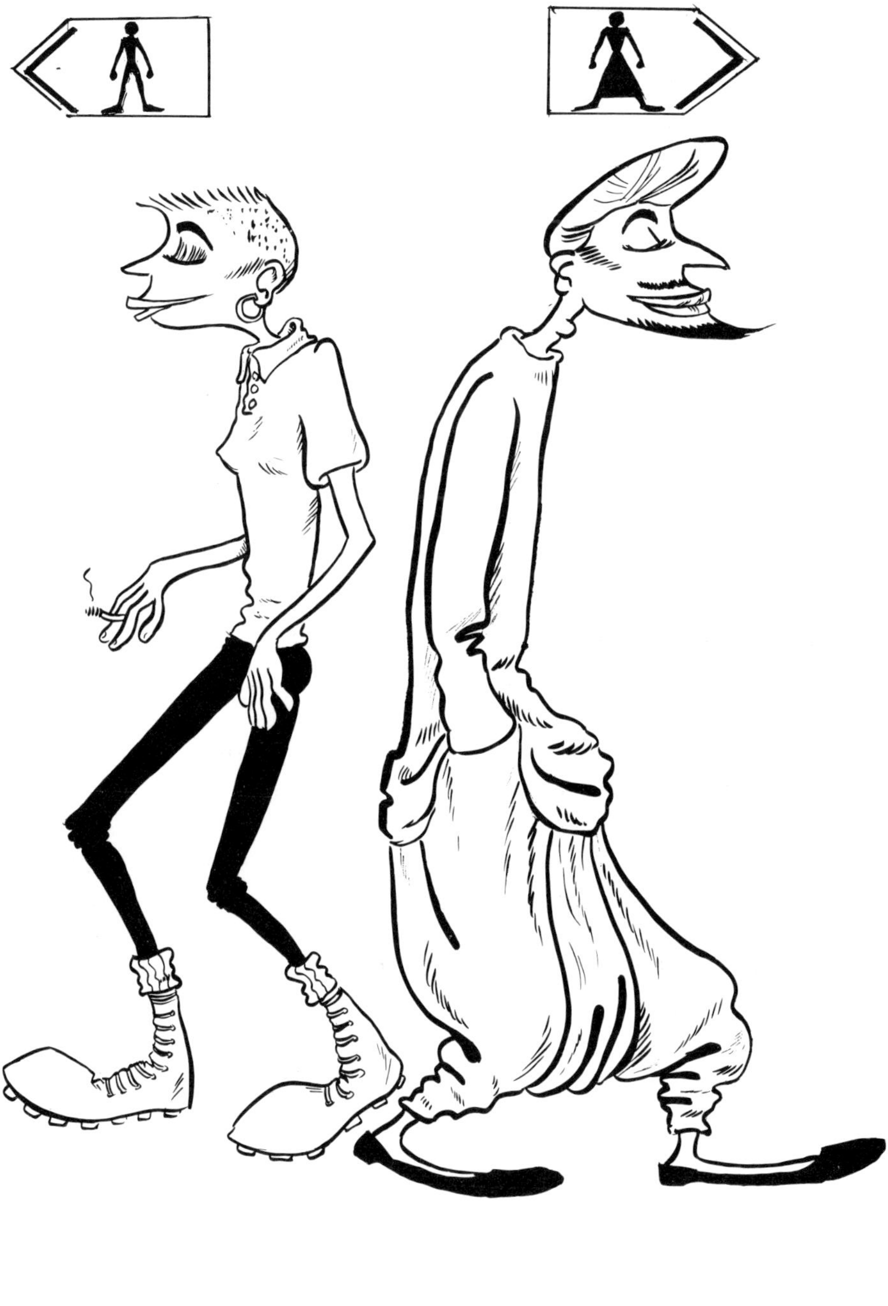

We bring memory to bear on what the painting gives us, filling in the gaps and interpreting details in the context of the whole. Because of this, an understated image can be more rewarding to study than one which tediously declares the obvious.

In *The Moroccans*, all that is not strictly necessary in design terms is left out of the image, just as a novelist might avoid describing irrelevant details of the furnishings of a room to prevent our being distracted from the action taking place within it.

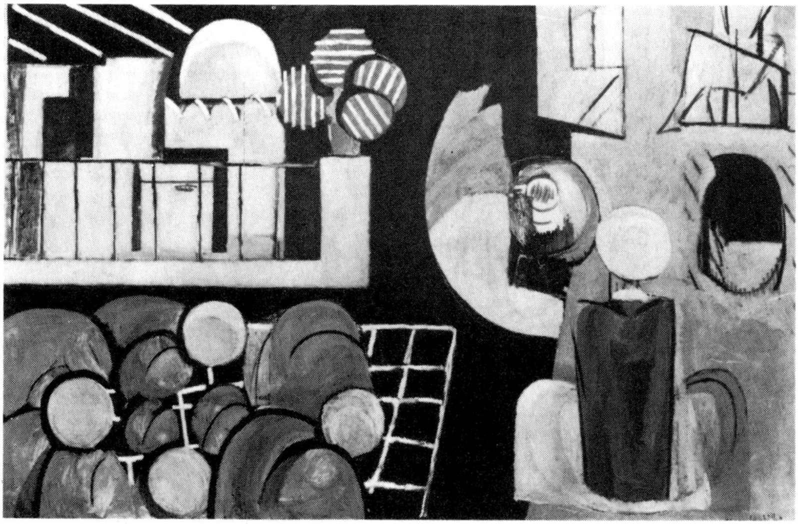

Henri Matisse *The Moroccans* 1916

Anything which does not play an active part is seen by the artist as a positive hindrance. Only those shapes which are in 'dialogue' with the other shapes are included. 'Dumb' or 'antisocial' forms — those that don't communicate with others or contribute towards the establishment of the whole arrangement — are excluded.

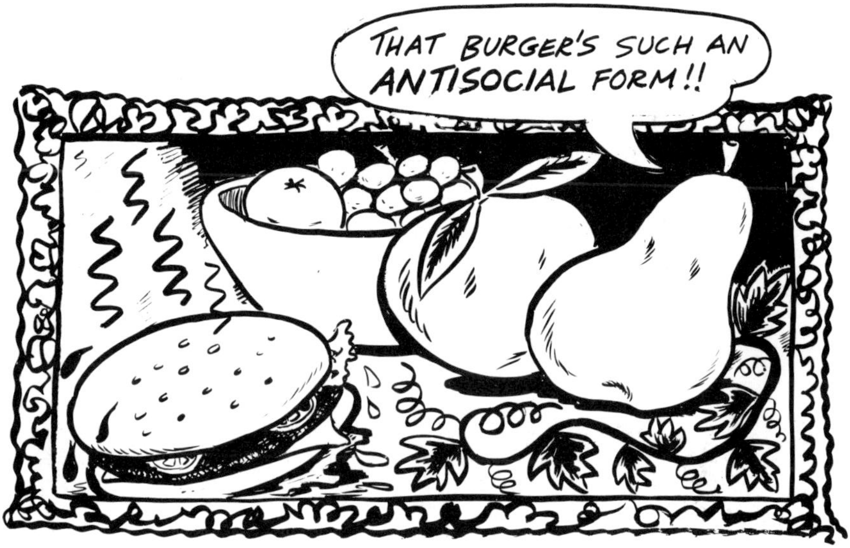

But Matisse avoids making his painting *too* simple. He has divided the canvas field into several distinct compartments before finding ways of reintegrating them into a unity. (Just as cards are shuffled before a game of patience, so that they can be reordered in the process of playing.)

'Visual rhyming' is again used as one way of creating links between shapes; of drawing analogies between different objects:

☐ The stylized circular forms of the pot of flowers on the balcony echo the shape of the head (seen from behind) of the turbaned figure on the right, as well as those of the melons in the left foreground.

☐ Given the painting's title, those melons and their leaves could also have been read as figures kneeling on a prayer mat.

Is this possibility of a double reading evidence of a vagueness, a *limitation* of Matisse's style? Not necessarily. Ambiguity could be viewed as a deliberate strategy for creating visual puns; for bringing richer associations into the work than would have been possible in a more detailed, literal style. Although the results may be relatively trivial here, this tactic has served greatly to increase the symbolic wealth of many other modern works of art. The loss of 'realistic' detail has been traded for gains in another field, and the language of modern art has been seen to contain possibilities not previously available.

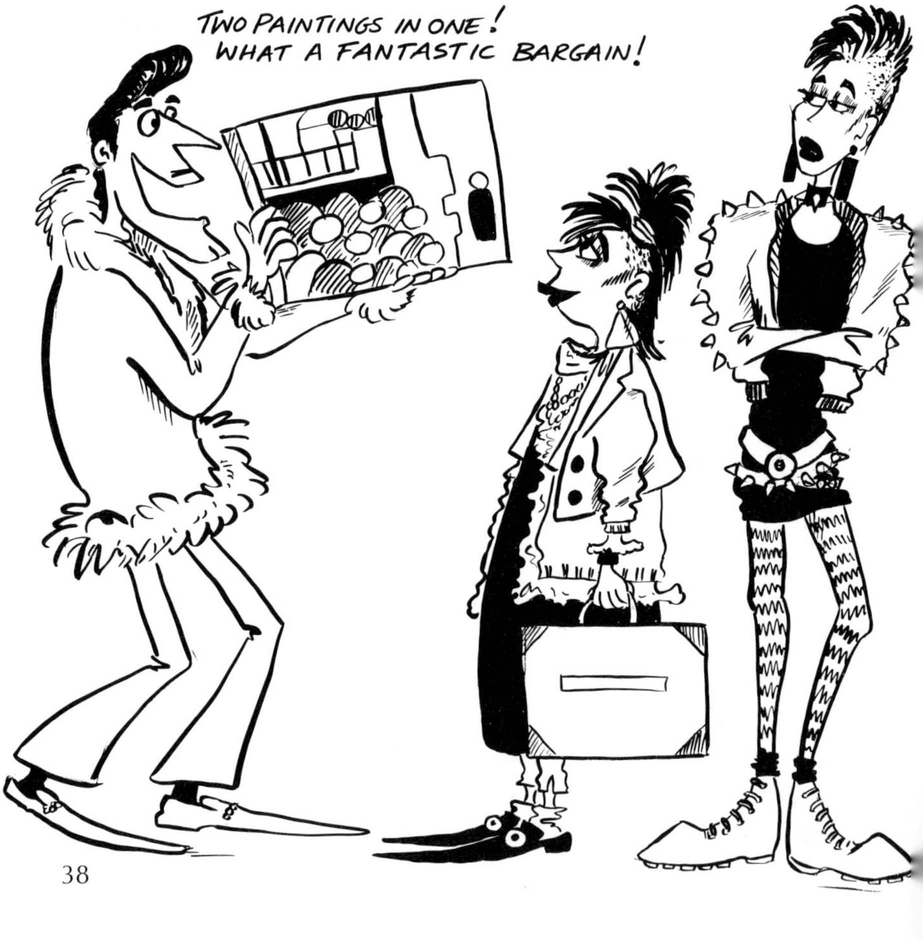

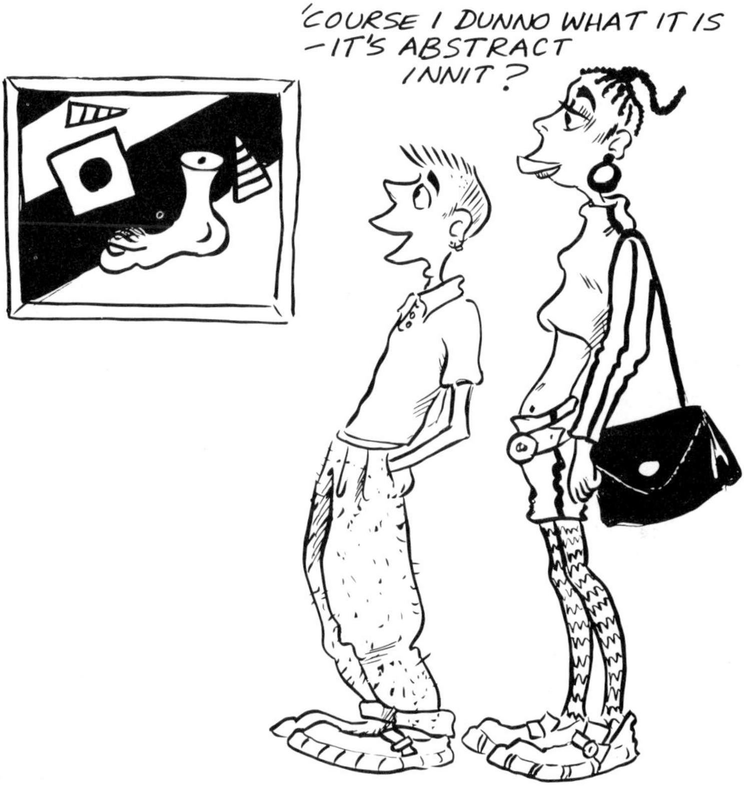

Abstract art — that is, art which appears to be concerned *only* with colours and shapes — is often seen as presenting particular problems of appreciation.

But rather than viewing it as a phenomenon apart from the rest of art, we can perhaps best treat it as an extreme case of the modern tendency to shift the emphasis away from resemblance and towards the formal language of art itself. On the one hand, as we have seen, no realistic art can avoid producing an abstract — a partial account — of the real world. On the other, no 'abstract' art can completely eliminate references to the world; it is impossible to prevent associations with reality.

It wasn't so much that, on its arrival, abstract art *created* a problem in the field of visual communication. The problem had already come into focus with the realisation by modern artists that art does not present a 'transparent' — an unmediated — image of the world. A crisis of representation already existed; abstract artists were among those offering responses to it.

Similar shifts were occurring in other areas of knowledge too:

In linguistics, for example, Saussure and others underlined the arbitrariness of the relationship that exists between words and what they refer to — between *signifiers* and *signifieds.*

In physics, Albert Einstein evolved his theory of Relativity which runs so much against our commonsense view of time and space: a world picture was created which our senses seem unable to confirm.

For several artists of this time, including the abstract painter Wassily Kandinsky, the conclusion to be drawn from the new science was that appearances could no longer be trusted. External reality was being recognised as unrepresentable.

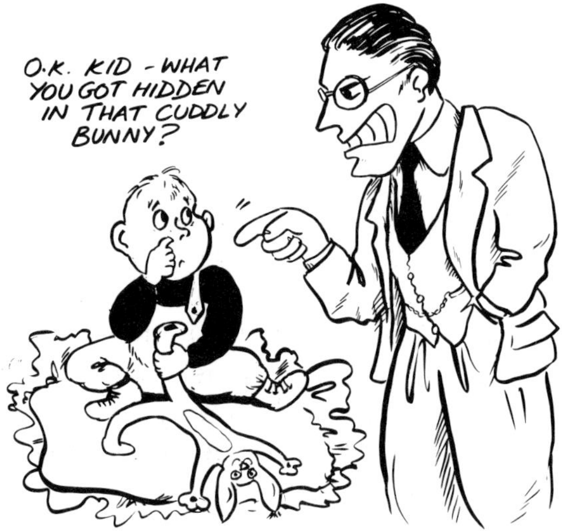

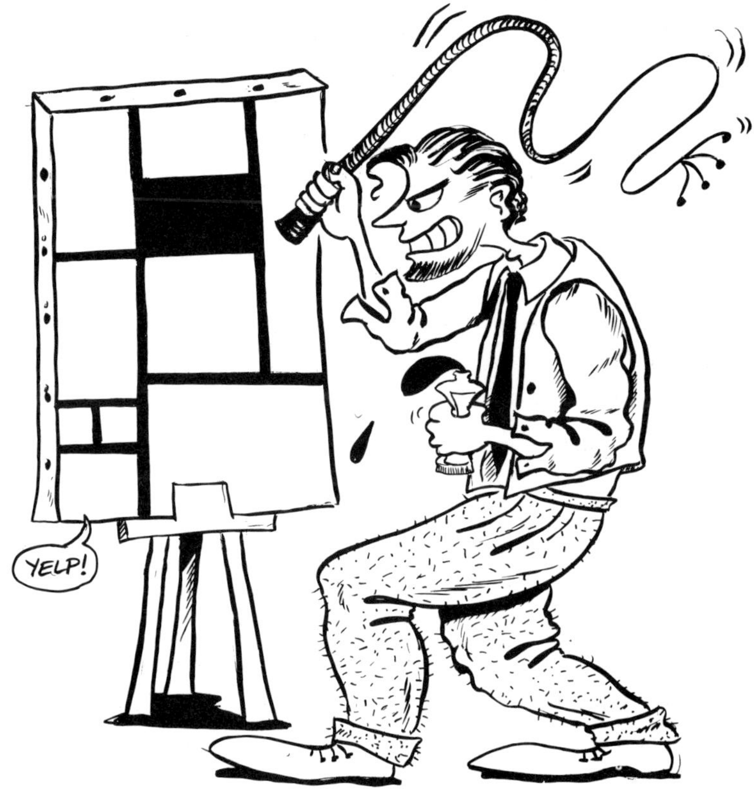

Starting anew in each painting and constructing with what he saw as the basic elements — vertical and horizontal black lines, together with squares and rectangles of red, yellow, blue (the three primary colours) or white — the concern of pioneer abstract artist Piet Mondrian was to create a harmony in more purely *visual* terms than art had previously been used to — to make the *forms* do more of the work.

His intention was to paint without a 'blueprint', to avoid being inhibited by the need to produce a resemblance to something in the natural world. Mondrian was not an artist to vary the style of his work just for the sake of novelty. Having 'purified' the language of painting to what he felt was its essential constituents, he retained the same building blocks in his art for about twenty years from the early 1920s until almost the end of his career. By consciously imposing limitations on the new and perhaps frightening freedoms (and responsibilities) his art gave him, Mondrian made it easier for spectators to become attuned to the subtleties of these unfamiliar compositions — to familiarize themselves with the conventions of his art, with the 'rules of the game' he was playing.

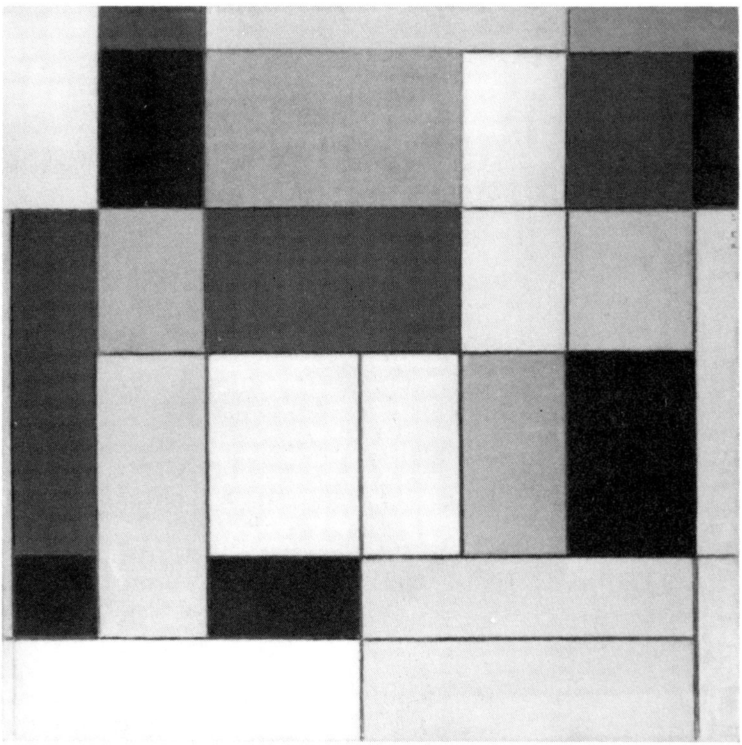

Piet Mondrian *Composition with Grey, Red, Yellow and Blue* 1920-6

For Mondrian, the inclusion of literal subject matter would merely be 'noise'. It would blur our awareness of the subtle adjustments he is making and hinder our appreciation that the true content of the painting is the harmony of its forms. As far as Mondrian was concerned, the basic issue was whether a painting 'worked' *as a painting.* Anecdotal subject matter, added onto the painting, might make it difficult to tell whether the forms were 'doing their job', and wouldn't ultimately compensate if they weren't.

Mondrian's notion of harmony is one of dynamic equilibrium. He is more concerned in his art with *relationships* than with things (even abstract things such as shapes). His paintings are not 'about' rectangles and lines; rather his conception of composition involves the establishment of a balance — an equivalence between diverse or opposing elements.

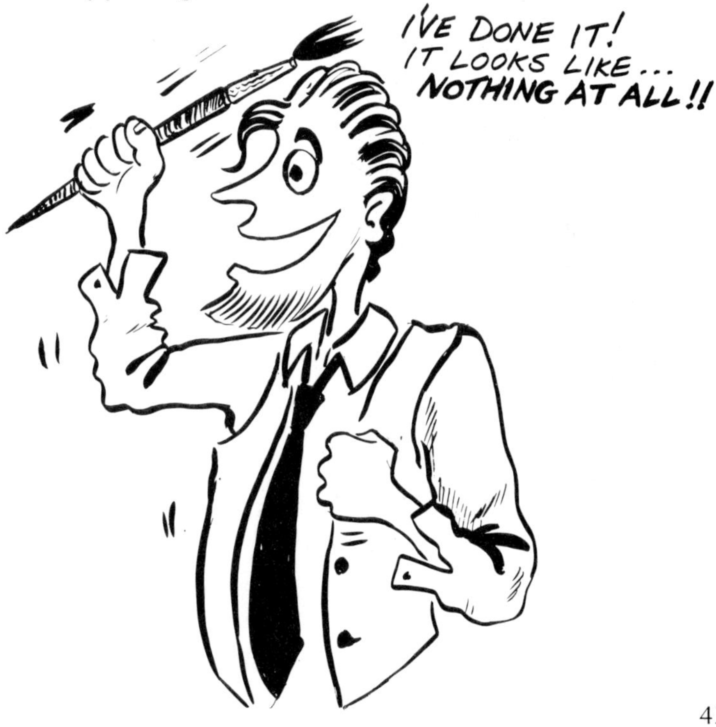

For instance, of all the lines available to him Mondrian selects only vertical or horizontal ones. By maximizing contrast, such lines allow oppositions of direction into the arena of the canvas in their simplest, most concentrated form.

Similarly, maximum opposition is also obtained by black and white, and by the choice of the three primary colours — those which contain no admixture of each other.

By echoing the edges of his habitually rectilinear (and usually square) canvases, the vertical and horizontal lines already perform a stabilizing function. In some of his later works, Mondrian feels the need to inject a greater dynamism by using a diamond format. Such a shape enables a more complex interplay between the edges of the canvas and the lines within it. To introduce diagonals *within* the picture would not have a comparable effect and would risk suggesting perspectival space which the restriction to verticals and horizontals prevents.

In certain works of the 1910s Mondrian experimented with grid-like structures, but he came to feel that the verticals and horizontals merely cancelled each other out, producing an easily-achieved, static order. The balance he sought in subsequent paintings called for a greater variation in the number, placement and indeed thickness of lines.

The various coloured areas of differing size are also balanced with each other and with the non-coloured areas (the black lines and the white spaces). Generally these 'empty' white areas need to be present in greater quantity in order to counter-balance the heavier, coloured areas (which themselves vary in weight: blue, for example, is denser than yellow).

Often the lines and shapes of Mondrian's paintings give the impression that they could extend beyond the boundary of the canvas edge.

Just as Cézanne's *Still Life with Fruitbowl* and Picasso's *Seated Nude* allow both two-dimensional and three-dimensional readings of their work, so Mondrian's images can be read both as flat designs on the plane of the canvas surface, and as having an undefined or unbounded space.

In the former reading (which the lack of modelling in the coloured areas contributes to) the whites are seen not as mere background but as positive parts of the two-dimensional design.

In the latter reading, the white areas seem to open out behind the lines (which themselves seem to burst out of the limited space within the frame). At the same time, the canvas plane appears to 'buckle' — since the yellow appears to advance optically, and the blue to recede.

The co-existence of these two readings — of expansion and limitation — established yet another dynamic opposition in the work.

Despite its geometric look there is nothing mathematical in Mondrian's art. His method of work had an intuitive aspect to it — adjustments were made during the process of painting as a result of feedback from how the images *looked*. As for so many other painters, it was important to him that his work was not merely a 'diagram' of a previously conceived idea. The eye, the hand, and the creative imagination — not just the intellect — had to be employed in bringing the work to completion; the initial conception evolved during execution.

Just as the creation of art has an intuitive aspect to it, so the appreciation of art must have one too. It could hardly be otherwise. The rules of composition cannot be reduced to an objective formula, or making a good work of art would be no different from doing a piece of arithmetic — you'd just have to get your sums right.

To introduce an idea of subjectivity like this is not the same as saying that 'anything goes', or that only those with some mysterious 'artistic sensibility' are able to appreciate painting. Notions of harmony have a conventional aspect, and although they may vary from artist to artist we can become attuned to them. It's rather like learning to ride a bike. Someone can give you hints, but experience — trial and error, doing it yourself — is

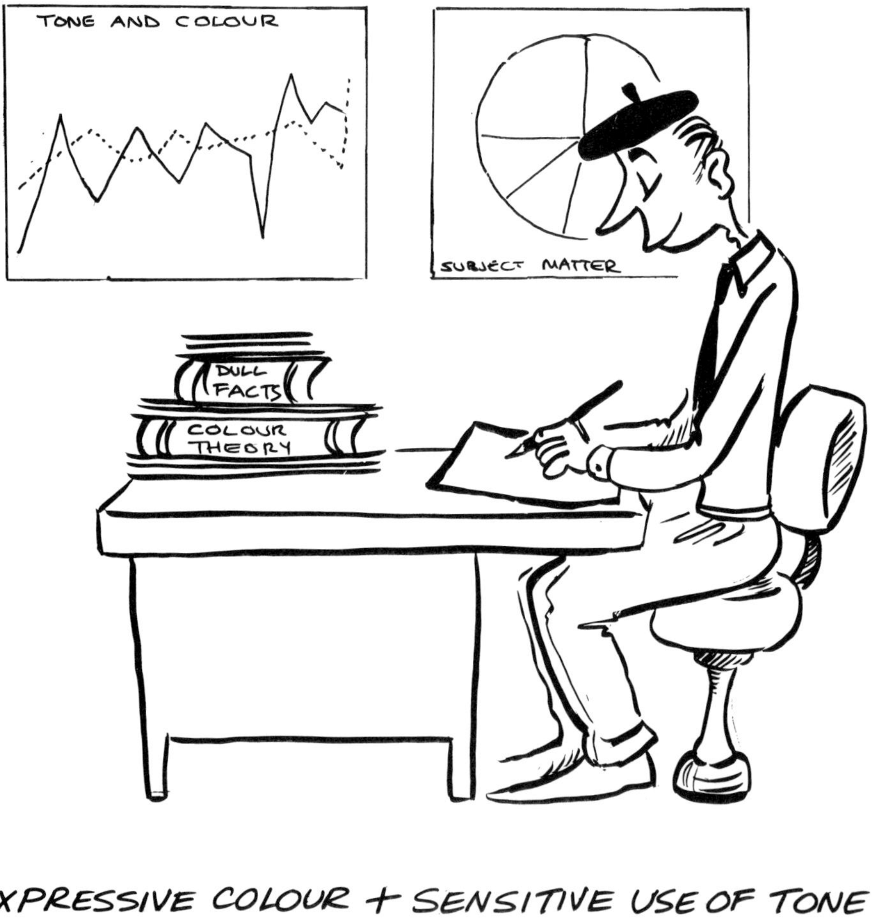

EXPRESSIVE COLOUR + SENSITIVE USE OF TONE

the only way to progress. All the factors involved in keeping your balance cannot be taken into account consciously, however real they are.

One way of testing out Mondrian's idea of compositional harmony would be to copy one of his paintings, but with some clear difference. For instance, would one of his paintings still 'work' if it were painted with white lines and black rectangles?

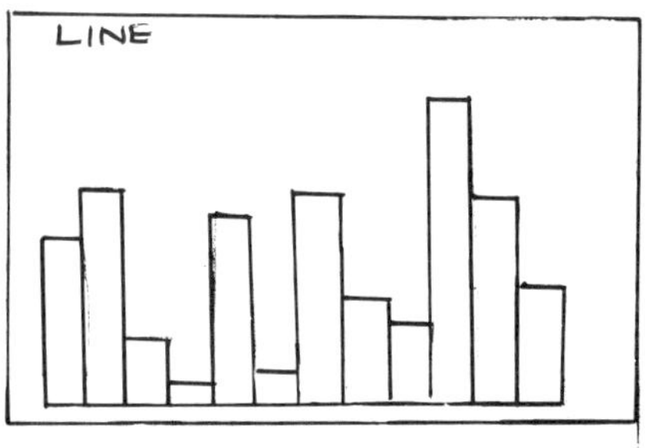

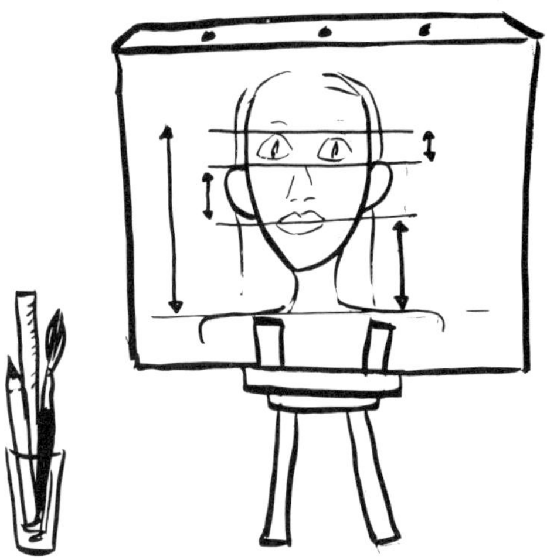

+ CLEAR LINEWORK = A MASTERPIECE!

Content

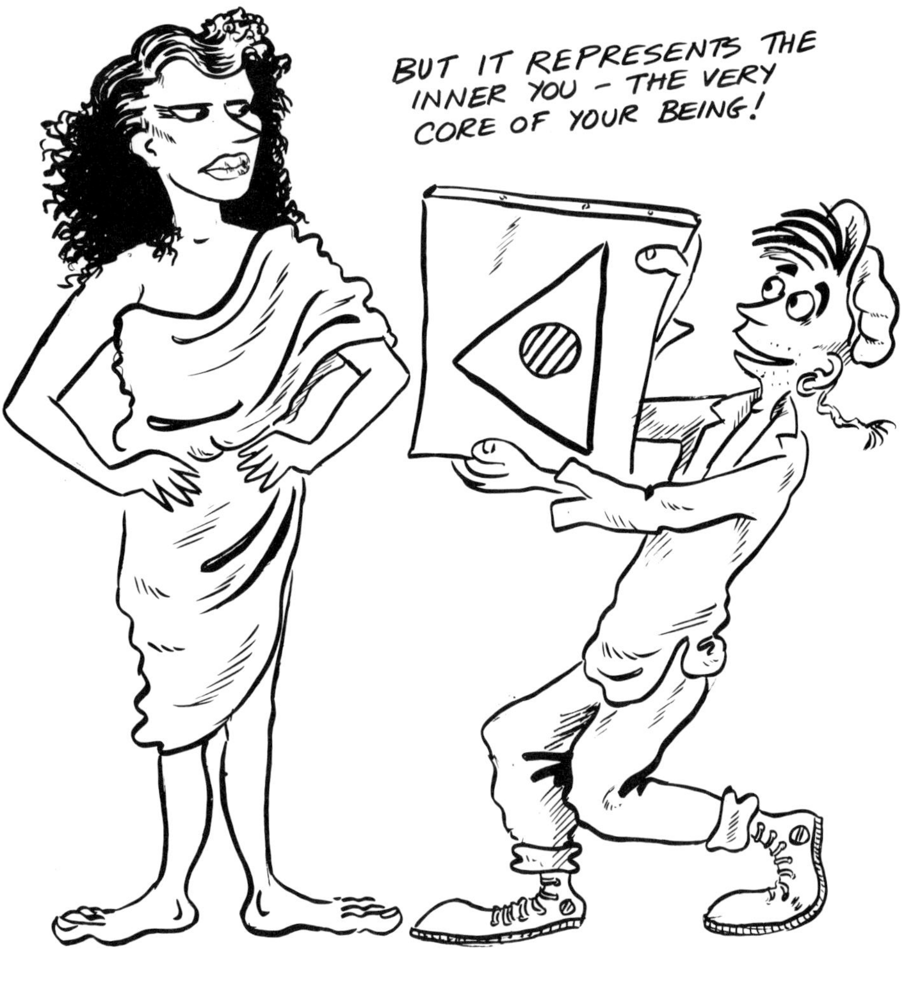

Since we've talked so much in these pages about a gap between art and life (and the consequent freedom of modern artists to concentrate on matters of form) perhaps it's worth emphasizing that modern art doesn't turn its back on reality altogether. Its independence is only a relative one. Although art ceases to be a servant of nature, tied to the creation of resemblances, much modern art still refers to the world. Moveover, the novel artistic languages it has developed enables life to be represented in new, often exciting and effective ways:

☐ The 'broken' brushstrokes of the Impressionists may be more prominent *as brushstrokes*, but they are also more effective than smooth academic brushwork for conveying atmospheric effects or reflections on the surface of water — aspects of nature the Impressionists were particularly interested in.

☐ The colours in Matisse's *Open Window, Collioure* may not be the ones we'd expect to find in nature, but they do evoke the feel of the hot, sunny weather of the south of France.

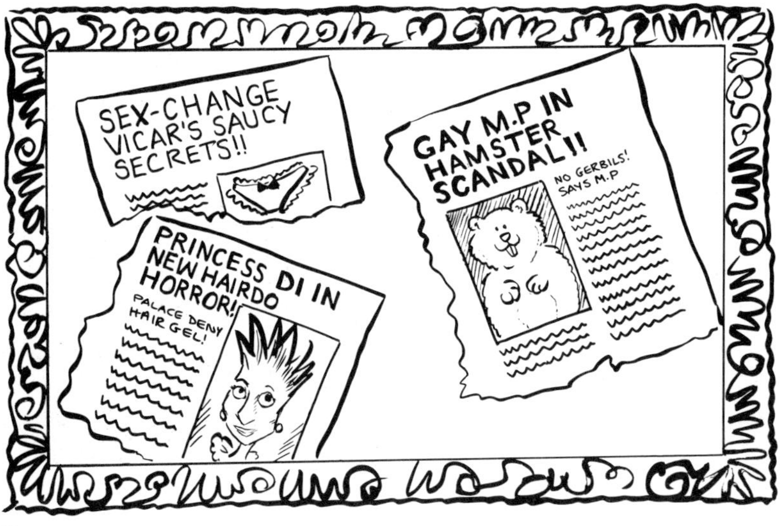

☐ And when Picasso felt his Cubist works were becoming too abstract, he began incorporating stencilled lettering to make them more 'legible' again. Later he 'collaged' (glued) pieces of newspaper and other materials for the same reason. Perhaps using a fragment of newspaper to represent a newspaper in a still life is about as 'realistic' as you can get, even if it is a modern technique.

Of course, some modern artists *have* consciously attempted to sever all links with reality, creating images that are intended to be nothing more than self-contained decorative objects.

In the paintings of Frank Stella, for instance, all the problems of representation that other modern painters have struggled with are left behind. Meaning is secure and unambiguous, but only because the formal elements do not attempt to *signify* anything at all — they merely represent *themselves*. Says Stella:

'My painting is based on the fact that only what can be seen there *is* there . . . All I want anyone to get out of my paintings . . . is the fact that you can see the whole idea without any confusion'.

Stella achieves an absolute clarity of content but only at the price of drastic reduction in the possibilities of communication, an elimination of art's ability to make references (including critical ones) to anything outside itself.

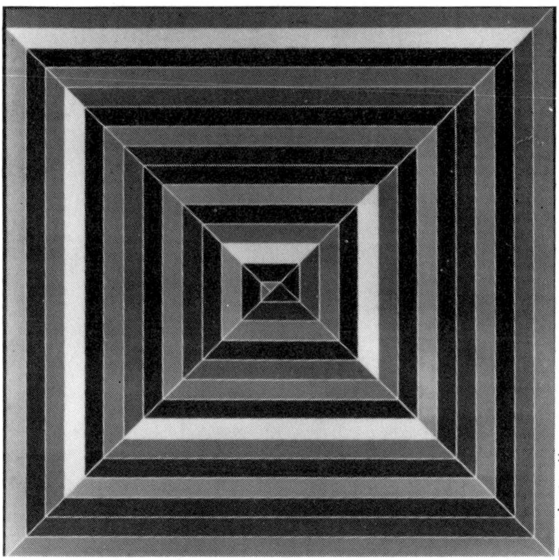

Frank Stella *Hyena Stomp* 1962

Despite what we might think, even in the realm of 'abstract' art this limiting position is not the norm. For Mondrian, for instance, the visual oppositions and resolutions of which his paintings consist are not intended to give us a solely sensory pleasure, to appeal to our fascination with the solution of pure design problems. Rather, this play with forms of is regard as embodying a symbolic content — enabling a reference to (what Mondrian believed to be) the nature of reality.

According to Mondrian, dynamic polarities — similar to what the Chinese call 'yin' and 'yang' — underlie all manifest reality, and can be seen for instance in the distinctions between male and female or mind and matter. Mondrian felt his art presented visual equivalents both to these interacting forces (he considered the vertical as 'masculine', the horizontal as 'feminine', for example) and — through its formal harmony — to the unity underlying nature's diversity.

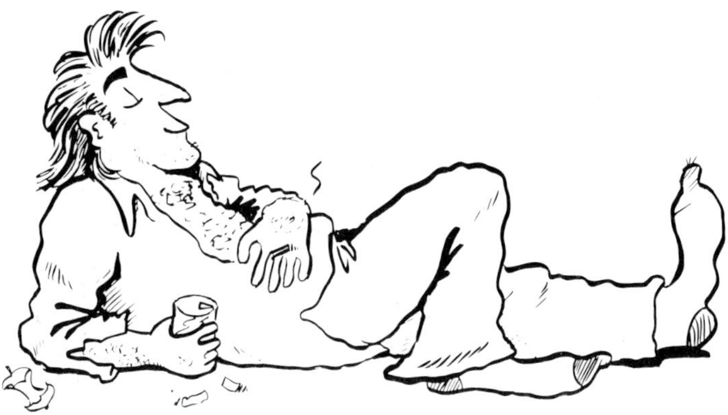

Mondrian didn't believe, then, that he was turning his back on nature in his art. True, he was not producing a catalogue of the particularities of natural appearance — the 'skin' of nature which the Impressionists so lovingly portrayed — but he felt that he was evoking a more universal, impersonal 'essence' of reality all the same.

The absence of visible brushwork in his paintings, or of any marked emotional tone, is an attempt on Mondrian's part to excise traces of individuality from the work — the artist's personal 'handwriting', as it were — in order that this 'objective' transpersonal reality might more fully be evoked. He knew that a totally impersonal painting would be impossible to achieve, but he wished to create a *balance* between the individual and the universal, the subjective and the objective.

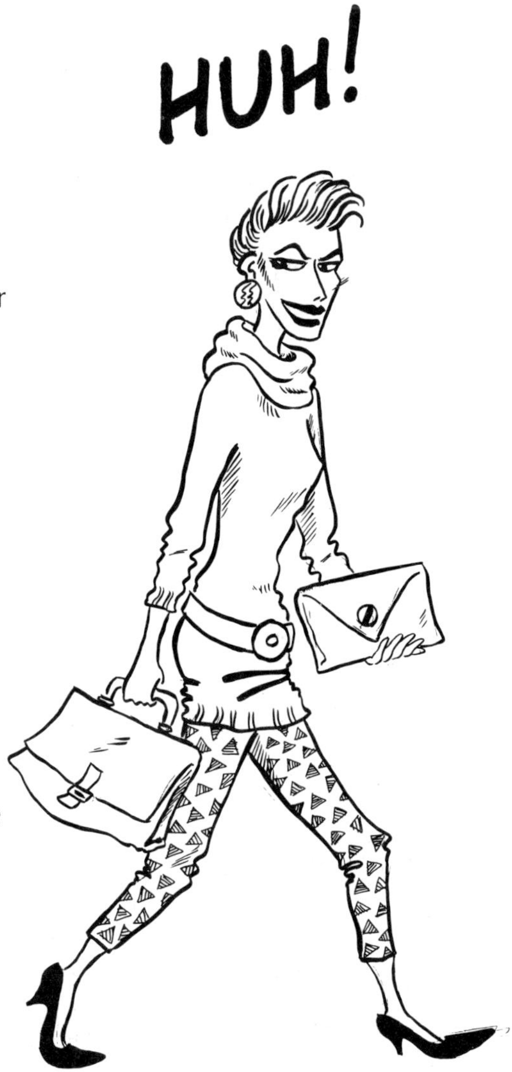

Mondrian was not abandoning reality; he was informing his work with a different notion of what 'the real' is — one derived from idealist philosophies. In such philosophies — Plato's would be an example — the world revealed to our senses is said to be an insubstantial one. Its forms have no separate existence in their own right, they are merely 'shadows' of a more real, invisible, spiritual being.

Although idealist world views seem always to have been with us in one form or another, they enjoyed a particular rise in popularity around the turn of the century. The work of many early abstractionists — such as the painter Kandinsky and the sculptor Constantin Brancusi — was underpinned by mystical or ideal notions of 'essences' or timeless absolutes.

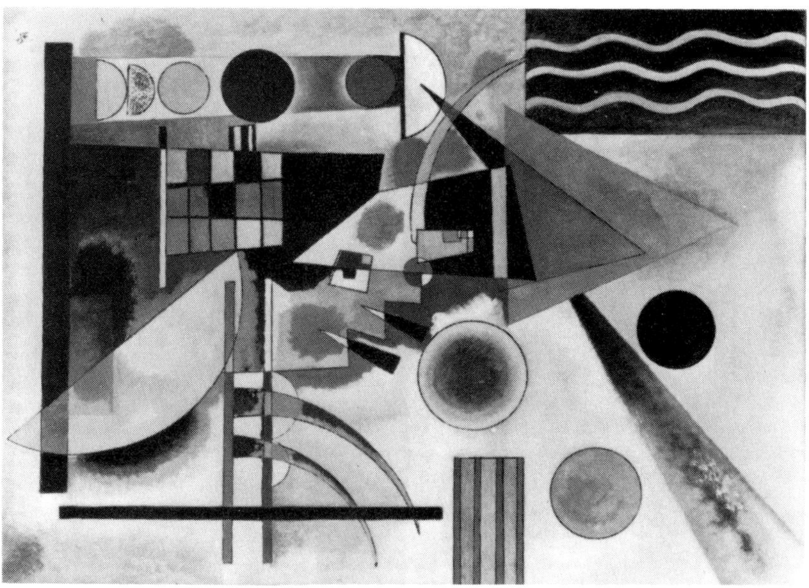

Wassily Kandinsky *Swinging* 1925

Idealist philosophies tend to encourage an inward-turning attitude: the mind should be led beyond an identification with the 'illusory' world of shifting sensory experience towards a oneness with Being. And it is in this process of spiritual awakening that Mondrian sees a role for art. He felt that his painting was able to present clearly to the spectator the dualities present in nature but normally 'veiled' from the senses due to the apparent multiplicity of forms that life can take. In its abstractness, art can stand above this confusion, leading the awareness upwards and imparting a knowledge that can then be used to get behind the veil of nature.

But what if we don't share Mondrian's (or Kandinsky's or Brancusi's) idealist metaphysics? Can abstract art still have any meaning for us? It seems to me that it could. Abstract art can be useful just *because* of its distance from the world — because its relationship to reality is clearly symbolic, and less that of an apparent copy.

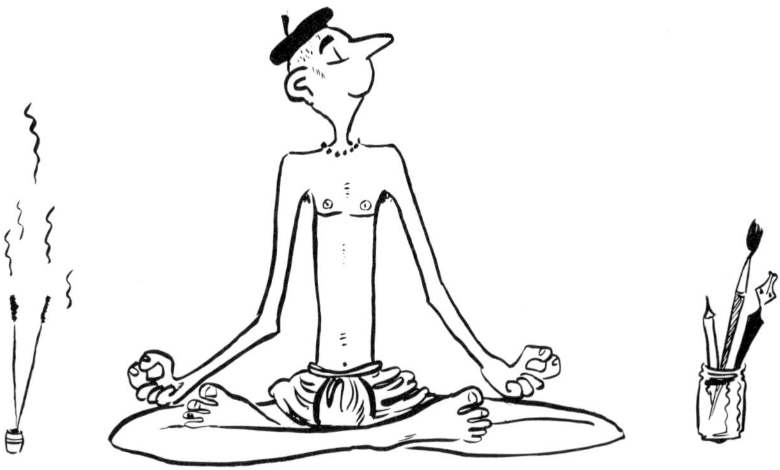

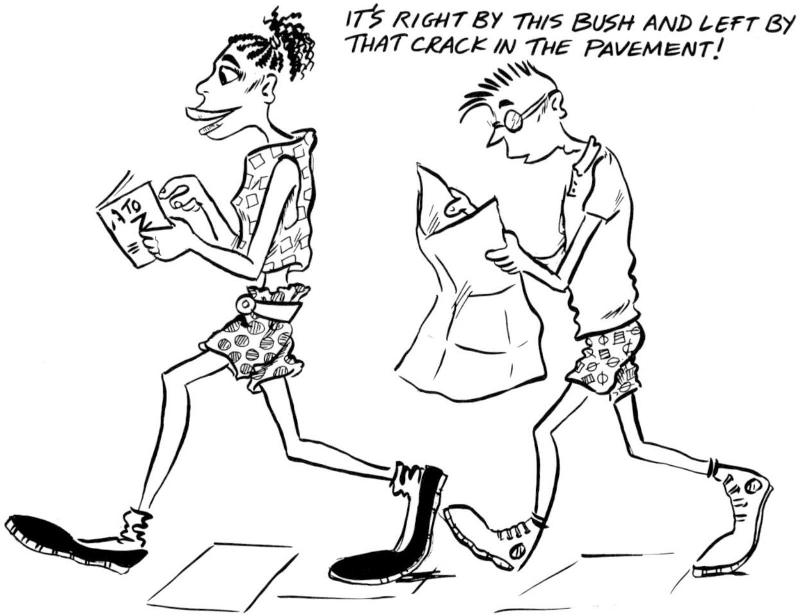

In this respect, a painting by Mondrian is analogous to a scientific equation (indeed, Mondrian himself refers to his concept of 'dynamic equilibrium' as a 'law of nature') or to a map. A map of London on the same scale as the city itself, or even one with an immense amount of detail — such as individual paving stones or leaves of trees — would be of very little use in finding your way around.

However abstract a map might be, there is a requirement that it encodes information about the world. And on some level, albeit a less strictly utilitarian one, abstract art must help us through the power of metaphor to represent the world as we envisage it, or aspects of our experience within it.

Art cannot provide a complete 'copy' of our visual experience. This problem of representation becomes more obvious when art attempts to image those aspects of life which are not visible. Idealists like Mondrian and Kandinsky believed in an unchanging invisible 'ground' of reality which art must attempt to evoke, but even to those who espouse a more materialistic world view there is clearly more to life than optical data reveals — there are sounds, emotions or concepts, for example.

An artist such as Frank Stella avoids the difficulties of representation by concerning himself solely with those aspects of the world that are themselves nothing but visual appearance — that is to say, shapes and colours (whose visible form *is* their substance). Other artists, however, take on the challenge of employing an abstract symbolic language to image life.

The Italian Futurist artists, for instance, attempted to represent the quality of 'dynamism', which they saw as a characteristic of the modern urban environment. But 'speed' is an abstraction that cannot adequately be

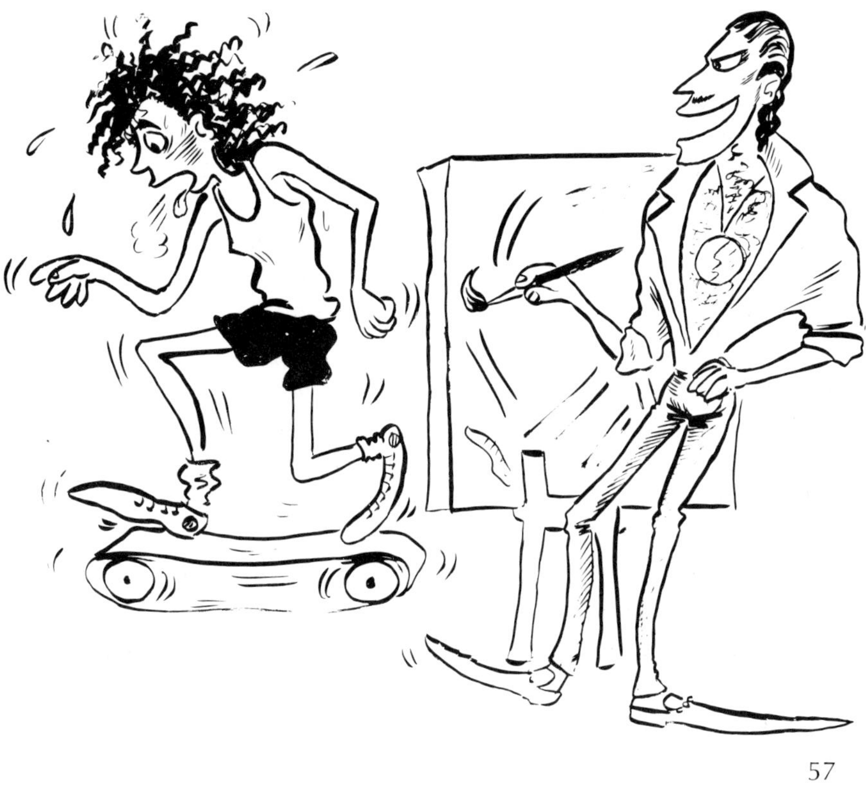

conveyed by imitative means within the static world of a painting or a sculpture, so the Futurists, such as Umberto Boccioni and Giacomo Balla, were naturally led towards an abstracted art where individual objects were often difficult to distinguish.

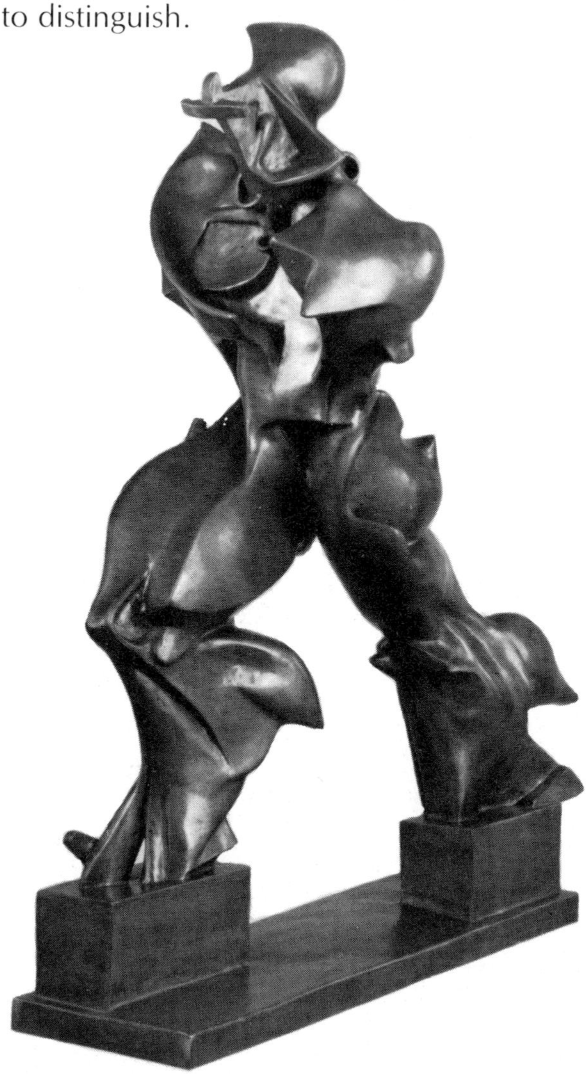

Umberto Boccioni *Unique Forms of Continuity in Space* 1913

In his poured abstract paintings of around 1950, Jackson Pollock is not so much turning his back on nature as employing a language that enables him to talk about the *processes* of nature — the (invisible) energy rather than the (visible) matter. Pollock's concern, he says, 'is with the rhythms of nature . . . I work from the inside out, like nature'. The world picture of interconnectedness and flux that his paintings embody has parallels with modern physics as well as with the more mystical world pictures of Oriental philosophy.

Pollock's paintings are not illustrations of some kinds of 'literary' subject matter. Their content has grown out of the play of paint and been fixed by the formal elements themselves, and it cannot be completely detached from them. For this reason it is difficult to talk about the content of such an abstract art.

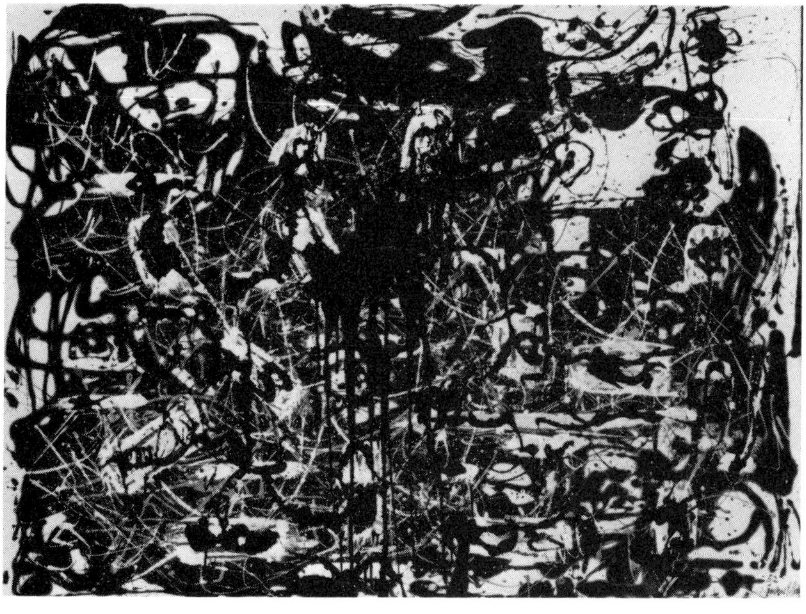

Jackson Pollock *Yellow Islands* 1952

Paintings of this kind are not necessarily 'vague' (as their critics might say), or 'ineffable' (as some supporters may claim). The problems begin when we attempt inappropriately to find direct verbal equivalents to visual representations.

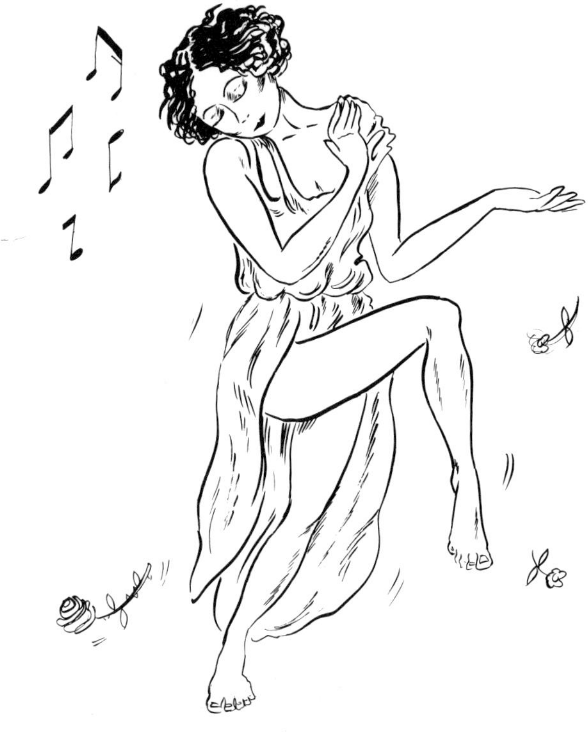

The dancer Isadora Duncan once said: 'If I could tell you what it meant, there would be no point in dancing it'. Her argument is that there are contents which can only be voiced through a particular channel of communication, and which would be 'injured' in the translation into another symbolic code. Producing a verbal, rational description of Pollock's content can make it sound too consciously willed, and can collapse the richness of its symbolism by over-favouring a single reading of it.

Abstract art such as Pollock's is often accused of being too private in its meaning, but this is a problem faced by innovative art of all kinds, and in all ages. New symbolic languages or novel visual metaphors can prompt us to reorganize our understanding of the world. But they perform this task only because of our unfamiliarity with the connections they make, and hence their meaning can be obscure or undefined.

Abstract art is not *innately* private — there is no insurmountable barrier to our comprehension of it. It is private only in the sense that not many people have learnt how to 'read it' (like certain American Indian languages with only a handful of speakers left alive).

What might start off as a relatively private code — an individually conceived 'mutation' — can become adopted into our public codes of communication if it proves useful and vivid. That is, if it is favoured by the users of the code, or those who are in a position to exert control over how we picture our world to ourselves.

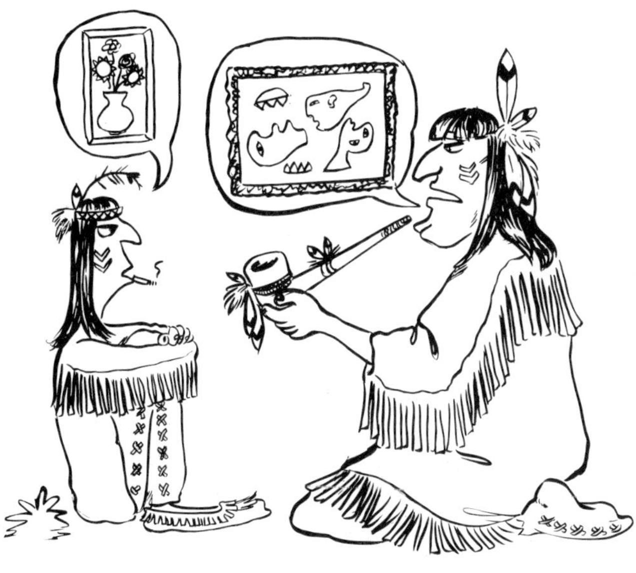

Much modern art has been more concerned with the expression of *feelings* than the description of things; a tendency that has been labelled 'Expressionism'.

For many modern artists the crucial inspiration is seen as coming from within, rather than from external reality. The painter Kandinsky, one of the most prominent of these Expressionist artists, talks for instance about 'inner

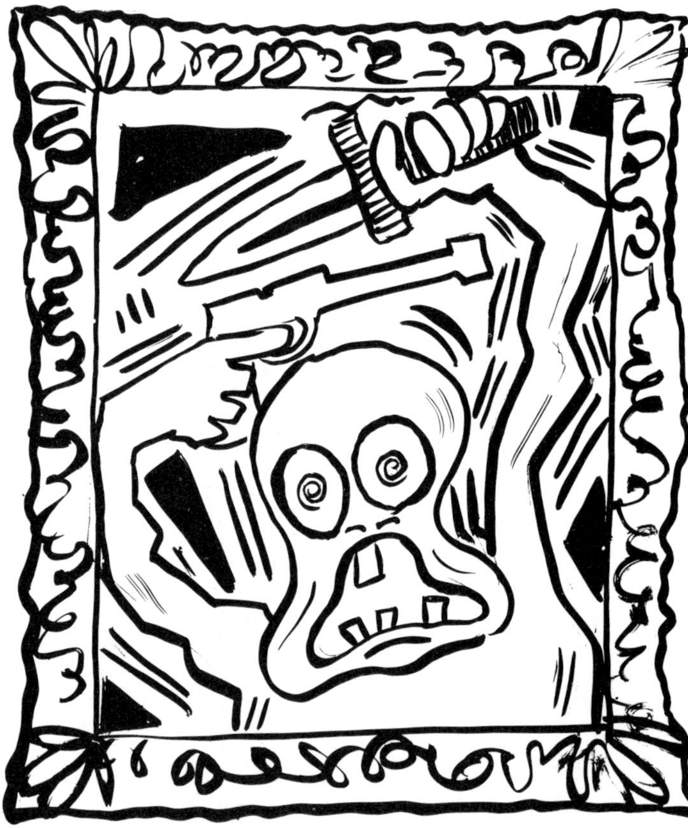

UTTER, TOTAL, AGONISINGLY HORRIBLE HOPELESS DESPAIR
Bernardo Disputtio 1984

necessity' as the impetus for all authentic art — some internal compulsion is seen as driving the artist to create.

The extremes of emotion provide the usual content of Expressionistic art. It attempts to reveal the state of the artist's soul, to convey the torments and ecstasies of the isolated modern spirit rather than the more commonplace emotions that are prompted by everyday social existence.

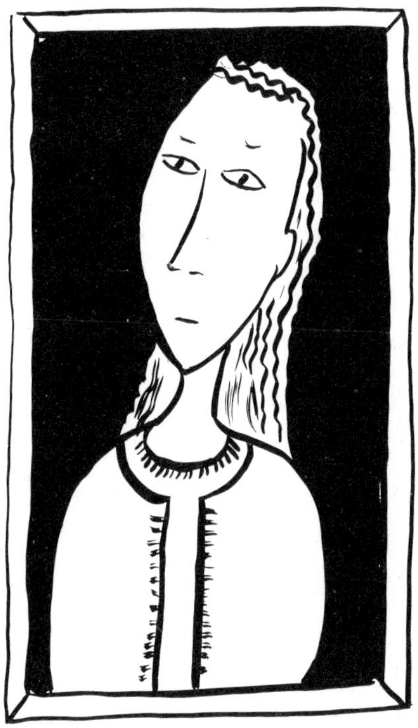

RATHER PEEVED

Brian Timson 1984

Indeed, Kandinsky sees his art not so much as a way of conveying personal feelings as of providing a channel whereby impersonal spiritual impulses might 'speak' through him.

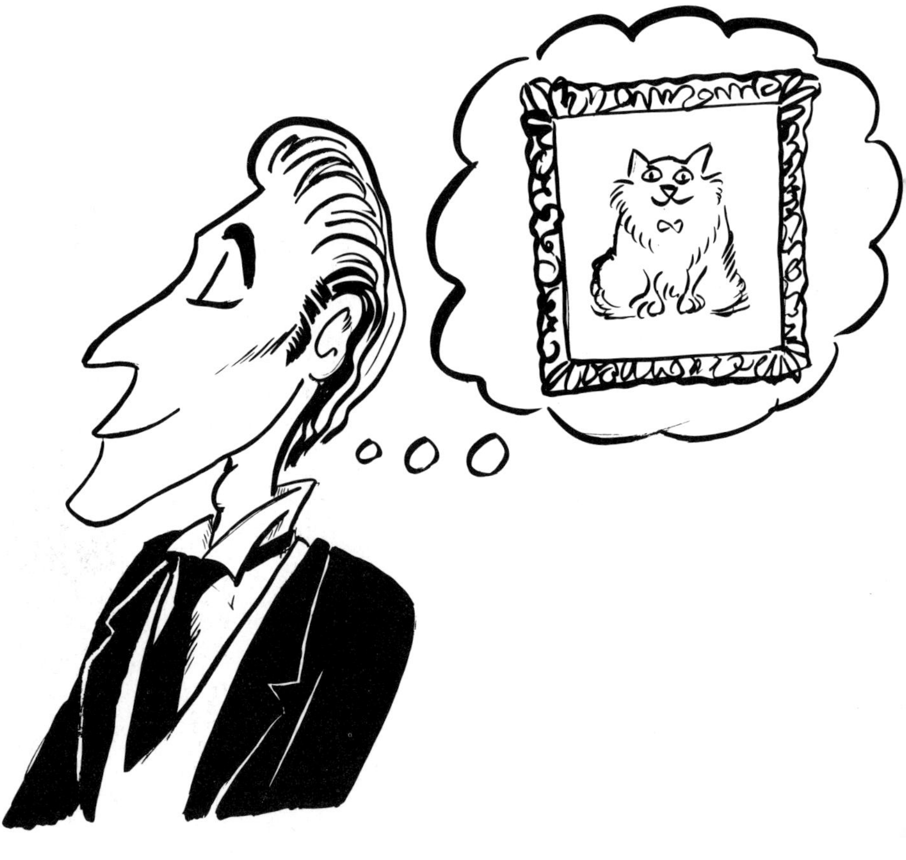

In its subjectivity Kandinsky's painting, like that of other Expressionists, is indebted to the heritage of the late 18th and early 19th century Romantic artists who often turned to the imagination as the source of their art. They regarded the inner world as more significant (and even more *real*) than the one presented to the senses. Here is the German Romantic painter Caspar David Friedrich talking:

'Close your bodily eye so that you may see your picture first with the spiritual eye. Then bring to the light of day that which you have seen in the darkness, so that it may react upon others from the outside inwards'.

In a sense *all* art — even the most descriptive in intention — must inevitably 'express' its creator, and earlier discussion should have made us wary of drawing sharp distinctions (as some critics have tried to do) between Expressionism and Impressionism. On the one hand no art innocently reflects nature, and on the other no 'expressionistic' art is completely without descriptive references.

Although there is no clearly defined break with the past, there *is* a tendency within modern art to give both a higher priority to expressing emotional states — as directly, spontaneously, and authentically as possible — and a belief that this expressive goal has to be achieved at the expense of precise description.

Clearly, feelings themselves cannot be directly described — we can decide what shape an apple is, but what shape is happiness?

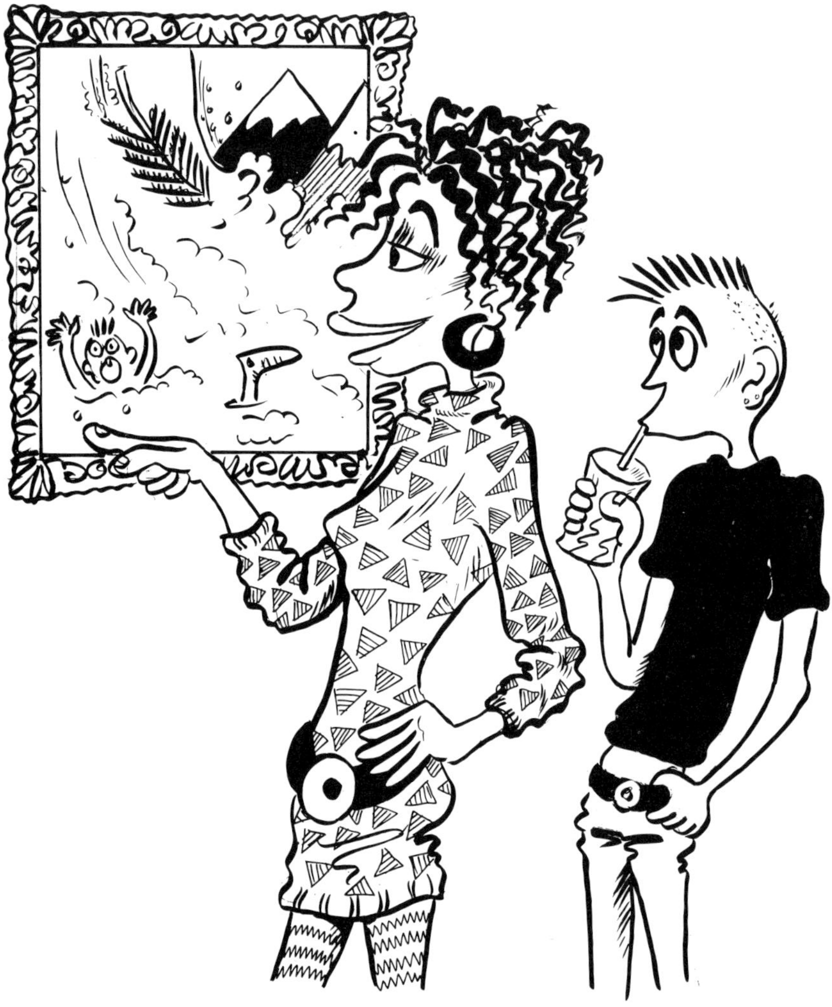

In earlier times, 'illusionistic' painters were able to suggest emotion in their works through the gestures and facial expressions of the figures, but this round-about method was not altogether satisfactory. Showing emotions being experienced (and even their cause) can't be relied on to recreate the same feelings in the spectator.

A painting of travellers being engulfed by an avalanche is hardly likely to evoke a sense of awe and terror in someone in the safety of an art gallery — unlike an avalanche in real life.

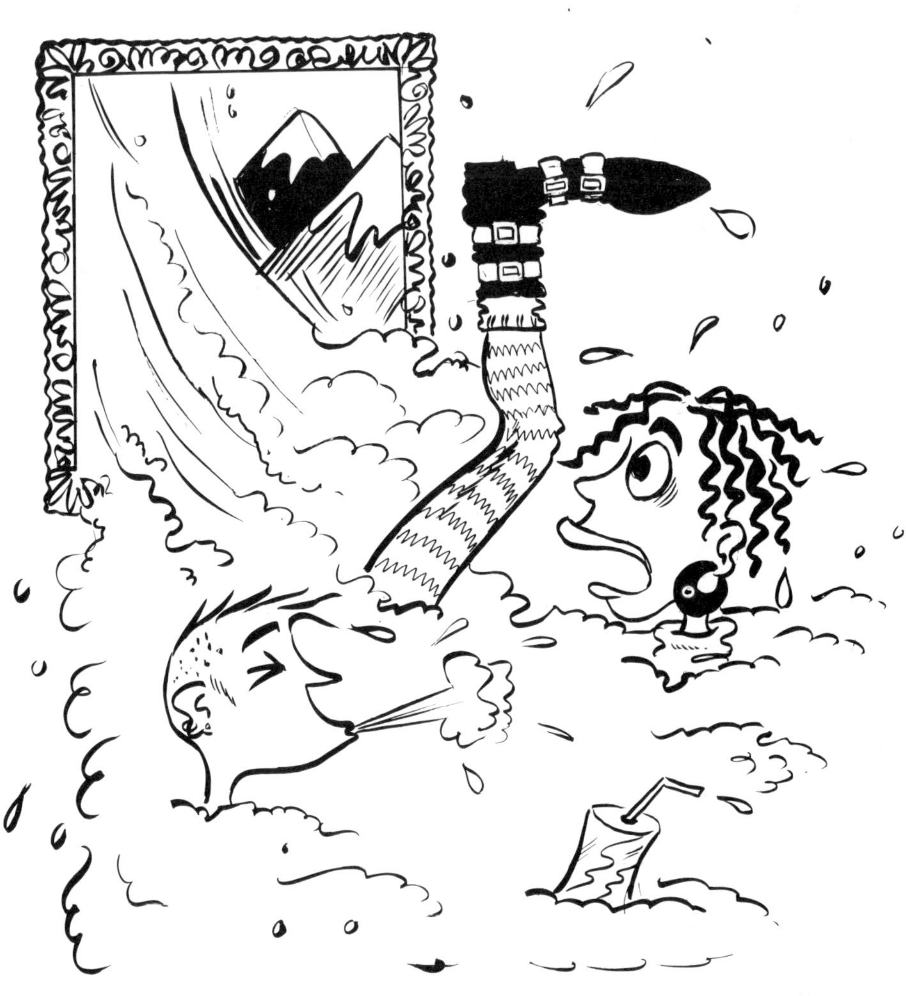

In Expressionist art, shapes are often distorted and colours heightened in comparison with what descriptive conventions might have led us to expect. This is done in the belief that emotions are more forcefully and directly expressed through a picture's forms than through its subject.

The intense colours and exaggerated perspective in Van Gogh's *All Night Café* of 1888 exemplify this tendency in modern art — indeed, he has been called the first Expressionist painter.

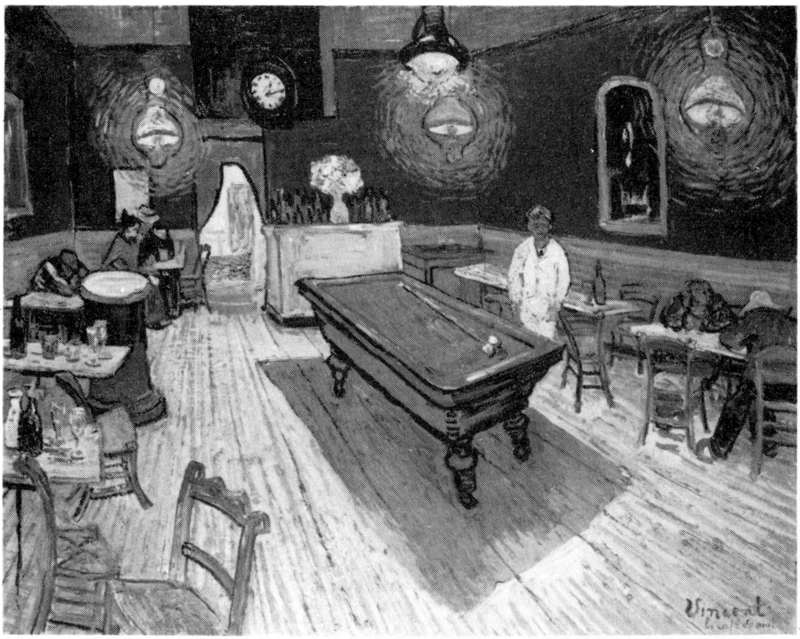

Vincent Van Gogh *All Night Café* 1888

Its distortions of shape and colour parallels a singer's exaggerated delivery of a song to imbue it with feeling — enunciation which would seem affected in everyday speech.

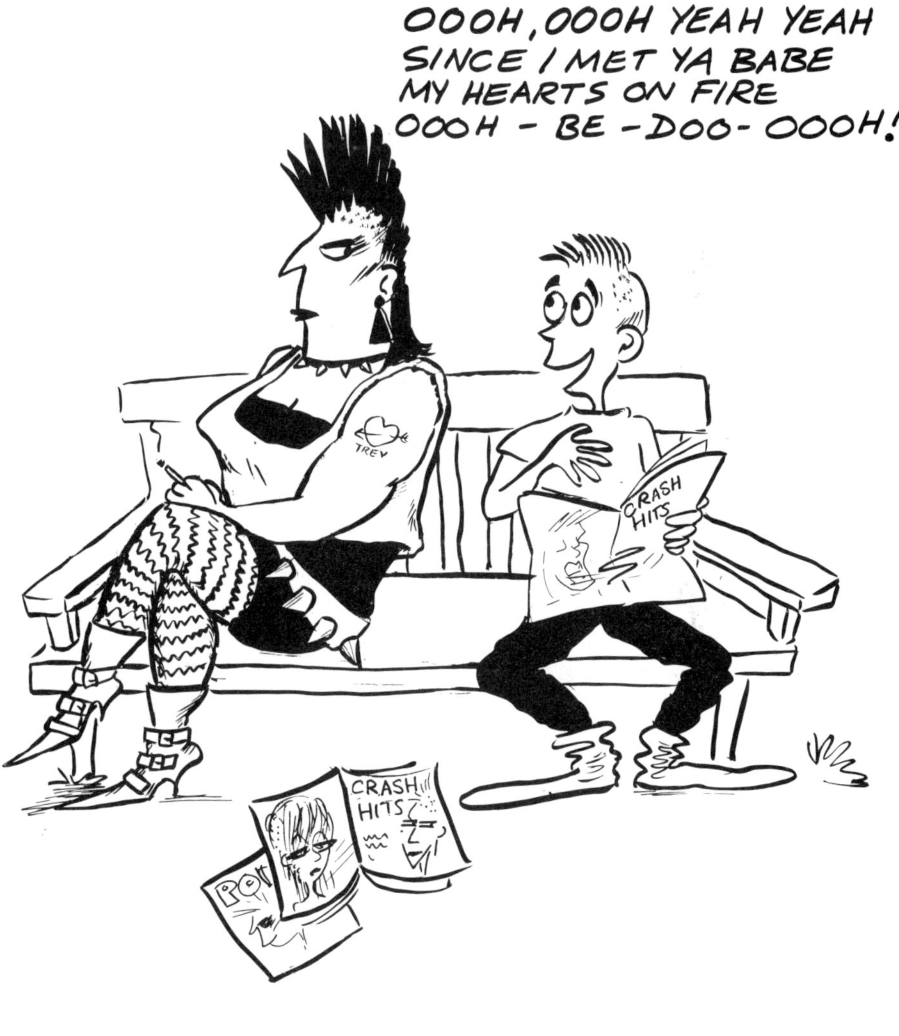

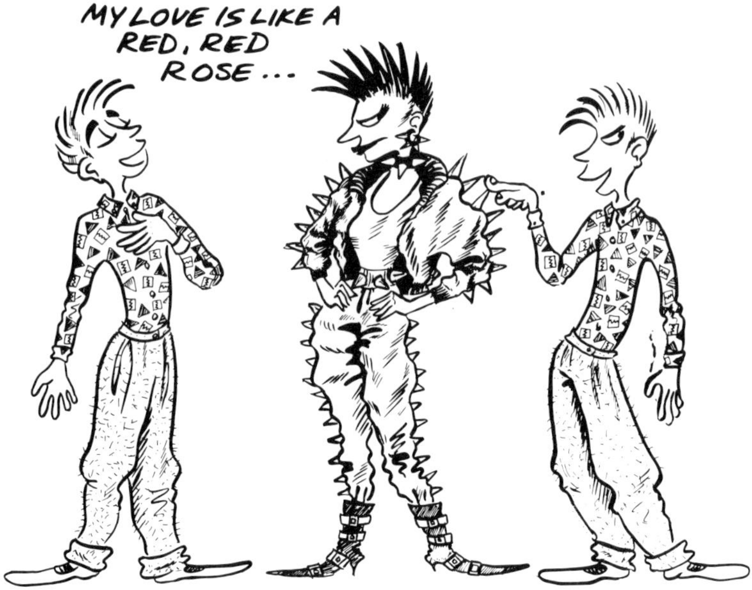

Another parallel lies in the extravagant metaphors of poetry. Or indeed of everyday conversation.

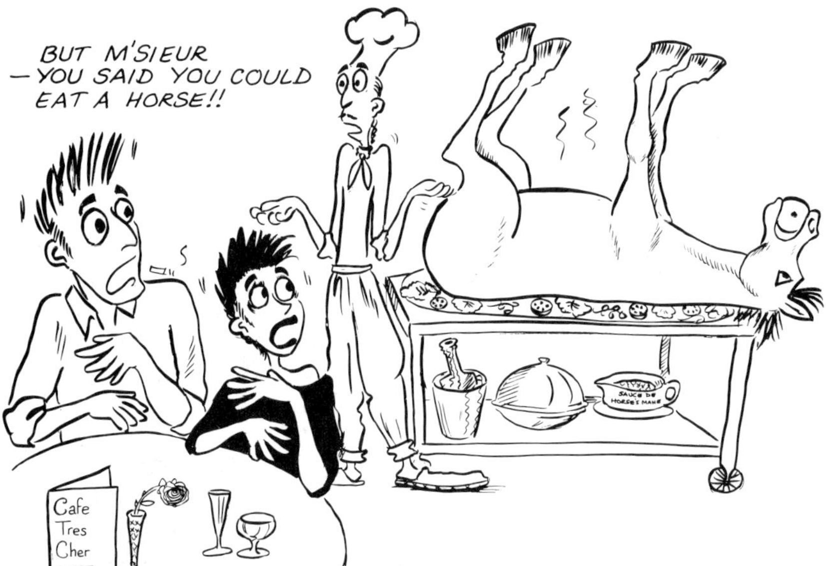

Such figures of speech give emphasis to our communication and it doesn't matter that they are not *literally* true — the effect on the listener is what counts.

The break with a descriptive mode is easier for modern artists because of their acute awareness of the conventionality of art. Once they accept art's need to create its own rules, they no longer have to worry about 'distortion'.

Expressionists abandoned the polite but dull formulas of 19th century academic art and sought inspiration elsewhere, for example in the simpler, stylized art of earlier eras, such as Gothic sculpture or medieval woodcuts — images which to their eyes appeared more emotive.

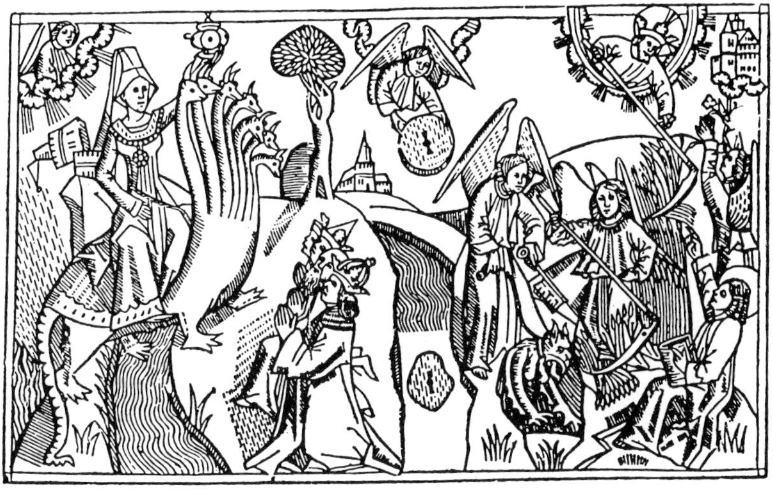

Whore of Babylon Nuremburg Bible 15th century

What distinguishes modern Expressionist artists from earlier painters who also attempted to convey moods is their belief that form — line, shape, colour, and so on — is capable of conveying expressive messages in its own right. In short, that form is itself part of content. Specific shapes and colours are believed to provide equivalents, symptoms, or translations, of particular feelings.

Because of the degree of autonomy the moderns believe art enjoys, they have a desire to find more purely *artistic* means of expression. 'Subject matter' (as traditionally understood) is often played-down. The content of a painting is secured in terms of paint — it is embedded in the visual elements themselves and not just illustrated by them.

Some Expressionist artists, including the mature Kandinsky, felt that conventional subject matter was superfluous — or worse, a positive hindrance — and this led them towards abstraction.

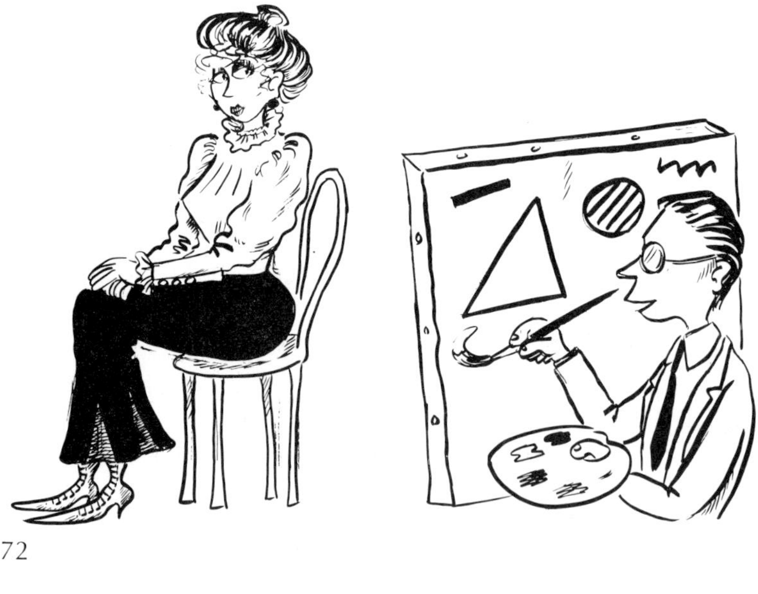

Emotion can be conveyed by form in art in much the same way as by tone of voice in speech. The same words can certainly be made to mean very different things by the way they are spoken.

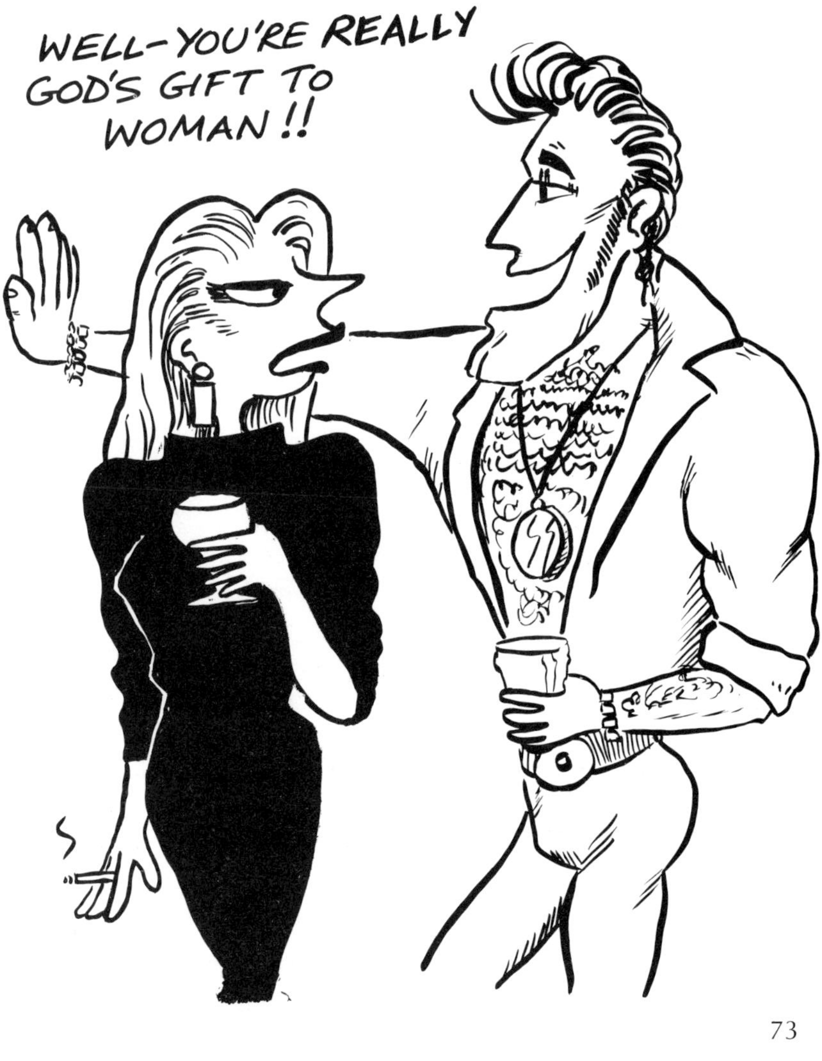

We would have no trouble, for instance, in appreciating the emotion being expressed by someone swearing in a foreign language. So it is clear how Expressionists could believe that form alone can convey meaning.

Analogies with areas outside art are not just of help to us as spectactors in learning to look at paintings; they have also been important to many artists of this century. In particular, music's abstractness — its ability to evoke mood without resorting to the description of everyday sounds — has provided a standard to which they aspired.

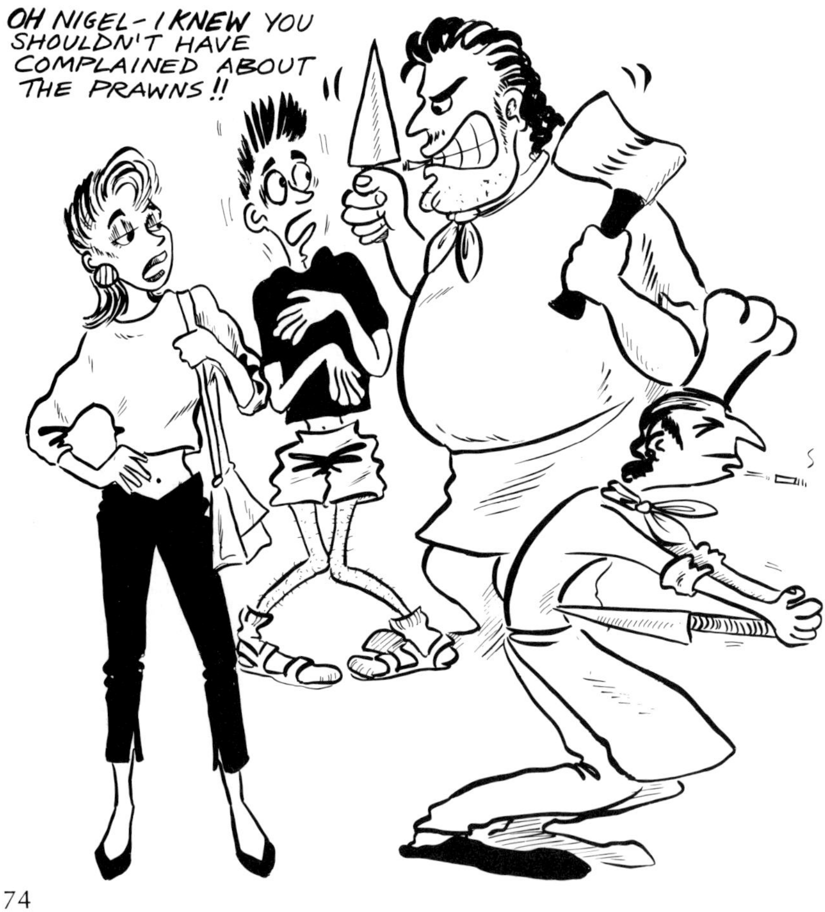

One key element in the Expressionist bag of tricks is line. No longer a servant to descriptive tasks, its role is not just to outline: it becomes a primary expressive means in its own right.

Concepts of 'precision' (more appropriate to technical drawing than art) are no longer relevant. Widely varying types of lines become available, reflecting not the artists' lack of the skill necessary to draw with more control, but their desire to exploit the range of options open to them — to use the whole keyboard, as it were.

To return to our analogy with the spoken word, an artist who insisted on always using a 'precise' line would be as boring as a speaker who said everything in a monotone. Or to put things in another way: a 'splashy' line *is* precise if it evokes the particular emotional nuance required.

Although most Expressionist painters tend to use line in an intuitive, spontaneous manner, some of them, including Kandinsky, tried to catalogue the effects that can be achieved with line, shape or colour. Georges Seurat, not usually counted an Expressionist artist, had already attempted this in the 1890s.

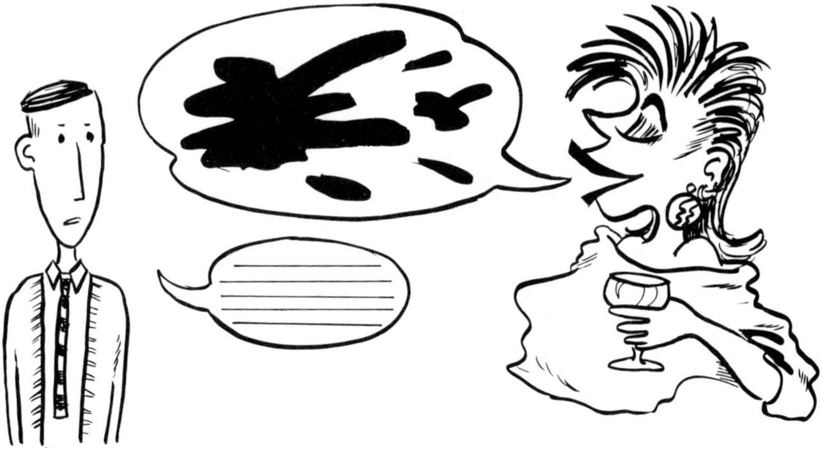

Seurat believed that when horizontal lines predominate in a picture a feeling of serenity is created.

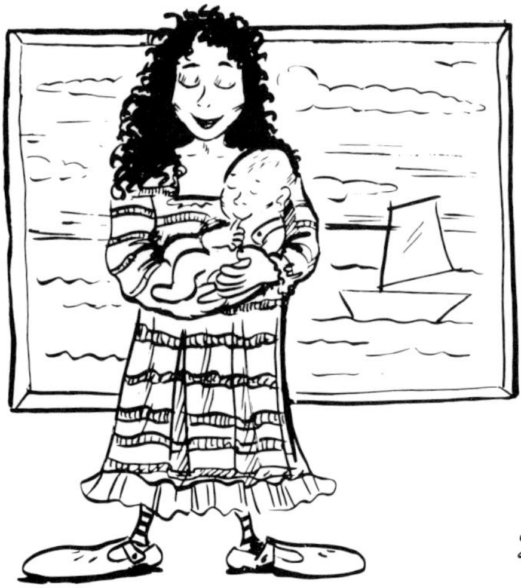

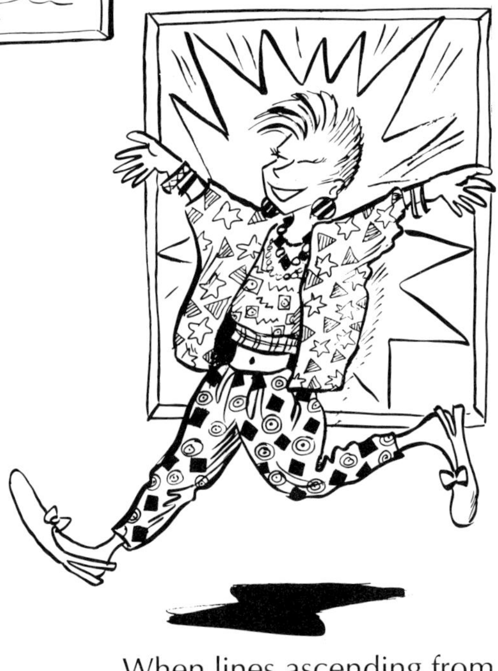

When lines ascending from the horizontal prevail, the sensation is one of gaiety.

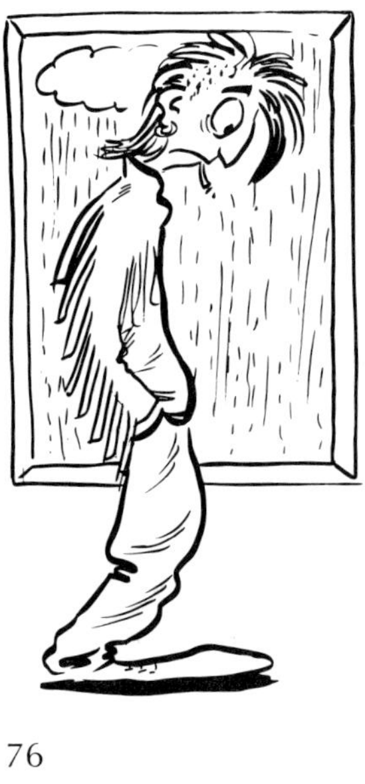

And when downward-moving lines triumph, there is sadness.

Line wasn't the only variable, of course. Seurat also associated sadness, for instance, with dark tones and 'cool' colours.

Paramount among the resources used by modern artists to express emotion has been *colour*. The academic artists of the 19th century had tended to neglect the importance of colour: their images were organized chiefly in terms of light and dark. In the hands of the Impressionists, however, colour gained a new status. Yet although they adopted a brighter palette — Monet even abandoning the use of black — they were not particularly concerned with the expressive use of colour. It was Van Gogh who played the key role in colour's liberation from imitative chores. Van Gogh explained his non-naturalistic use of colour in this way:

'I use colour arbitrarily to express myself more vigorously'.

Of *All Night Café* he said:

'It is colour not locally true from the point of view of the delusive realist, but colour suggesting some emotion of an ardent temperament.'

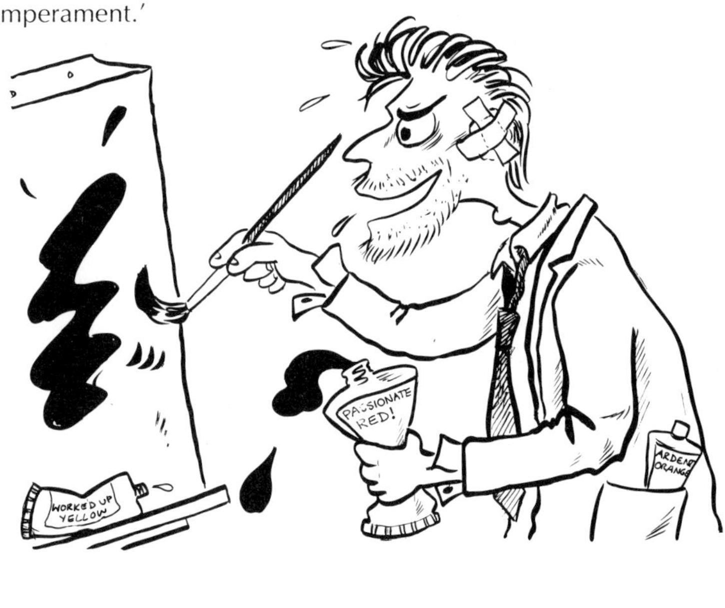

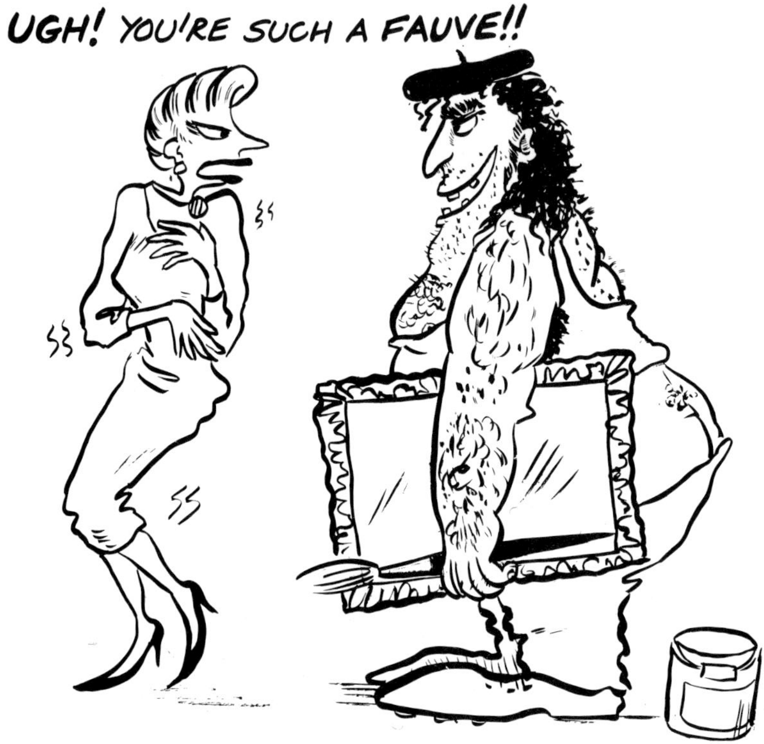

The Fauve group of painters represents the next flowering of Expressionism, coming to public notice around 1905. Matisse was the most important of the group, but André Derain and Maurice Vlaminck were also significant members of the circle. The Fauves (the name means 'wild beast' in French) extended Van Gogh's experiments with bright, non-naturalistic colour, spontaneously applied, and were influenced by Paul Gauguin's more decorative but equally intense palette.

Expressionism also flourished in early 20th century Germany (indeed, the word 'Expressionism' is sometimes used specifically to label this German school). The Brücke ('Bridge') group of artists (who included Ernst Ludwig Kirchner) began the tendency, with Kandinsky later producing perhaps the first abstract Expressionist works. These German painters were much indebted to the example of the Fauves, although Van Gogh's work also influenced them directly.

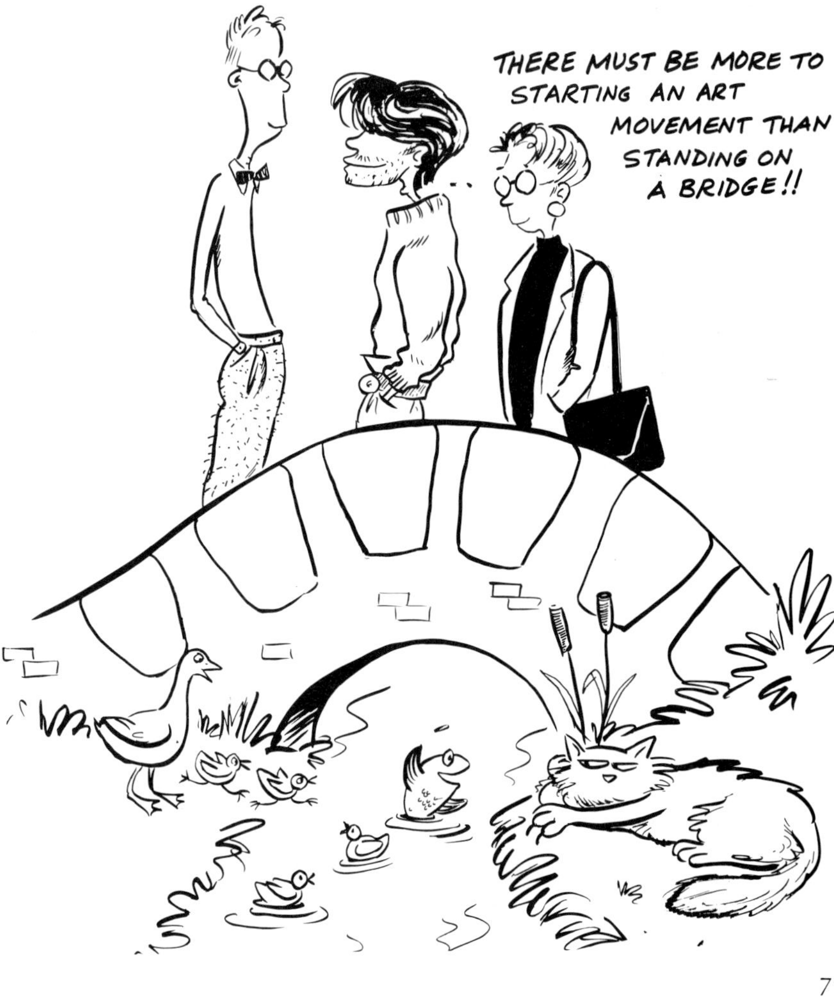

We can appreciate more clearly colour's potential for conveying mood by comparing its use in different works.

Vlaminck's *Red Trees* of 1906-7 depends largely on pure, primary colours, whereas Matisse's *Open Window, Collioure* makes much use of mixed tints and frequently employs white (either on its own, or to qualify the other hues). The result is a warmer and more light-hearted feel.

Kirchner's *Bathers at Moritzburg* of around 1910 possesses a less immediately pleasing, less harmonious colour than the Matisse. It has a more 'acidic' feel that contributes to a sense of heightened mood which is also quite different from that of the Vlaminck.

This distinction between the Vlaminck and the Kirchner is in some ways analogous to the difference between a major and a minor key in music. Less tinged by the Impressionist heritage which had no doubt affected the French Fauve painters, Kirchner produced a work which, though indifferent to the evocation of atmospheric effects, seems to glow from within with its own unnatural light.

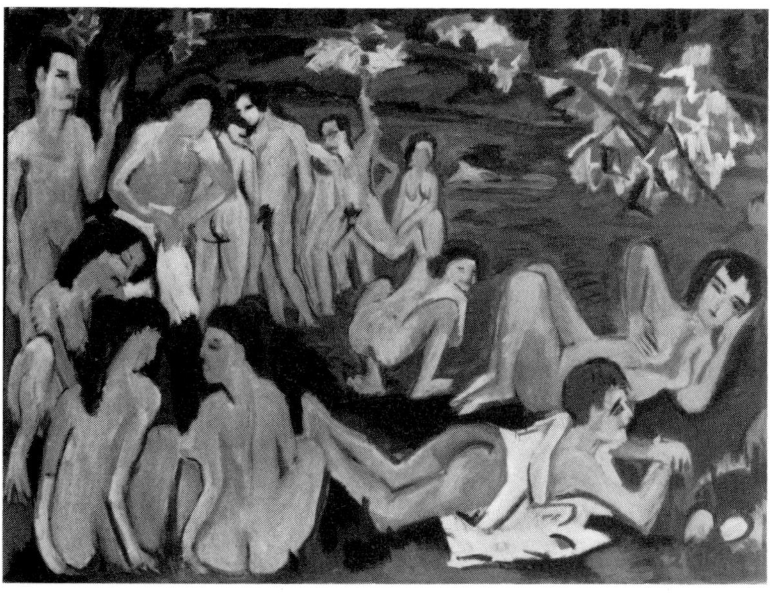

Ernst Ludwig Kirchner *Bathers at Moritzburg* 1910-20

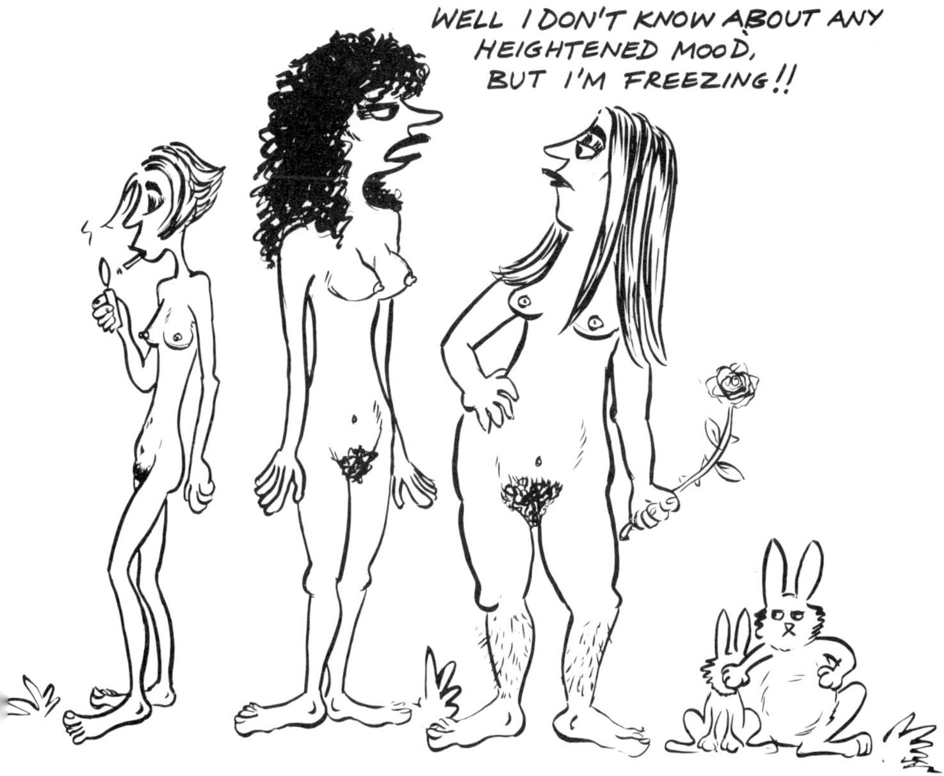

Despite its intensity, Vlaminck's colour is still derived to some degree from external nature: red tree trunks, for example, are a heightening — an exaggeration — of their usual brown. The greater abstraction, then, of artists such as Kandinsky shows a determination to use colour purely for expressive purposes. This priority given to expression determines not only the selection of colours but also the choice and arrangement of lines and shapes — and this accounts for some of the differences between his work and Mondrian's, where the placement of forms is determined more by the desire to construct a harmonious composition.

Van Gogh's use of colour is much more basic than that of later artists such as Kandinsky. *All Night Café,* for example, relies on the simple opposition of the complementaries red and green, by means of which he says he hopes 'to express the terrible passions of humanity'. Prettiness of colouring is avoided because it would establish the wrong mood. 'The picture is one of the ugliest I have done', Van Gogh declares. 'I have tried to express the idea that the café is a place where one can ruin oneself, go mad or commit a crime.'

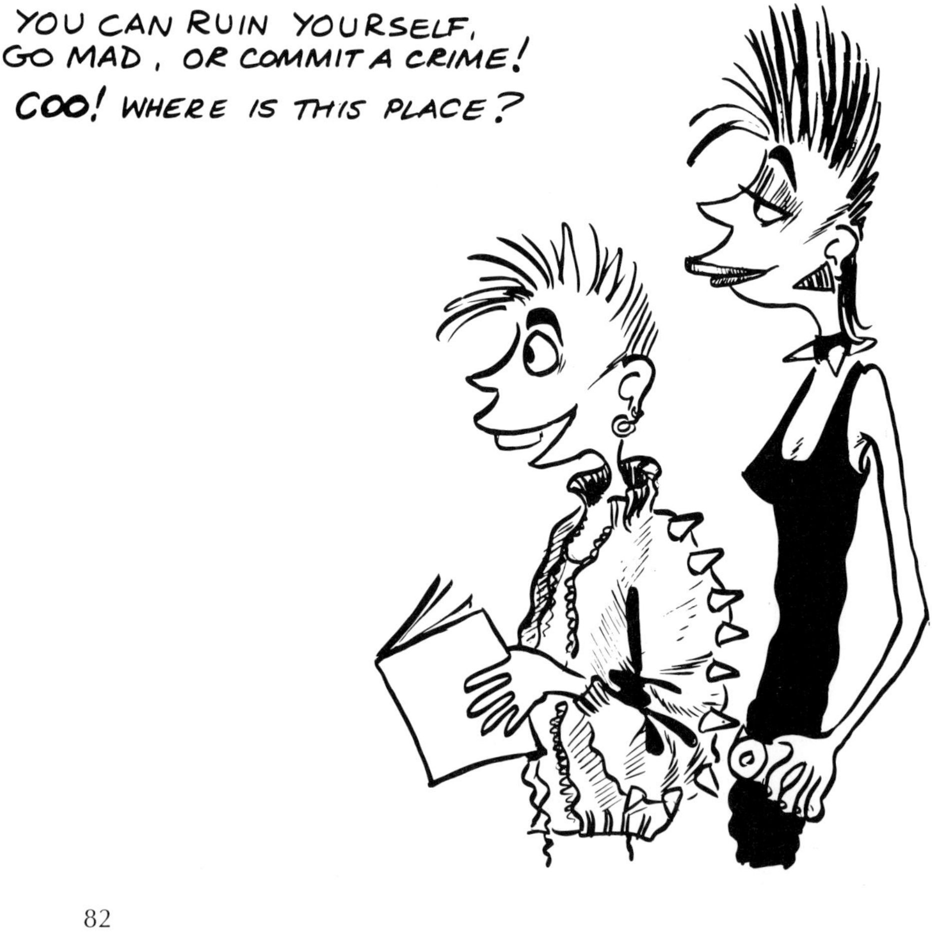

Of course, the idea that colour can correspond to mood is a commonplace of everyday figures of speech.

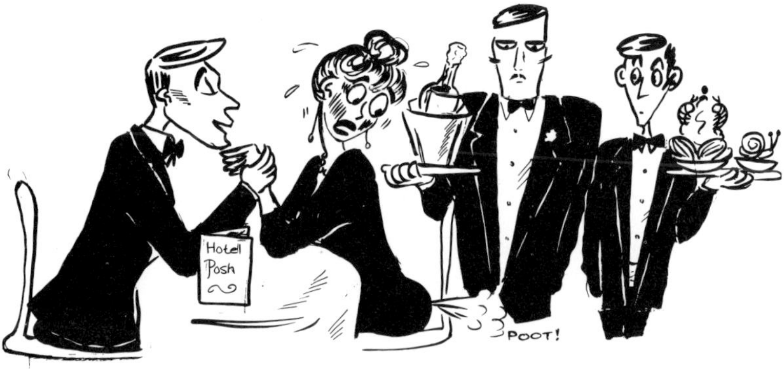

RED WITH EMBARRASSMENT...

WHITE WITH FEAR...

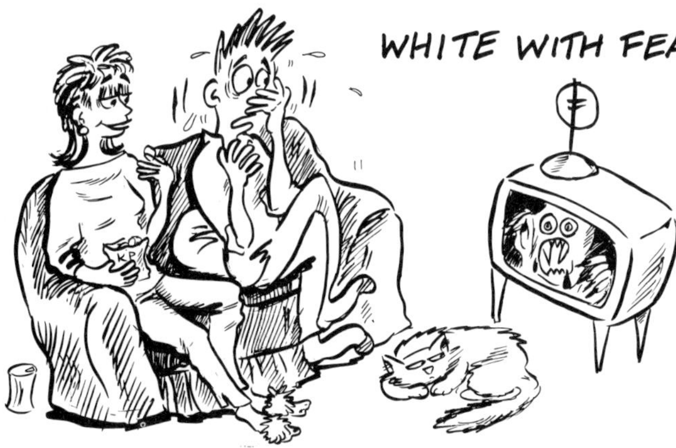

FEELING BLUE...

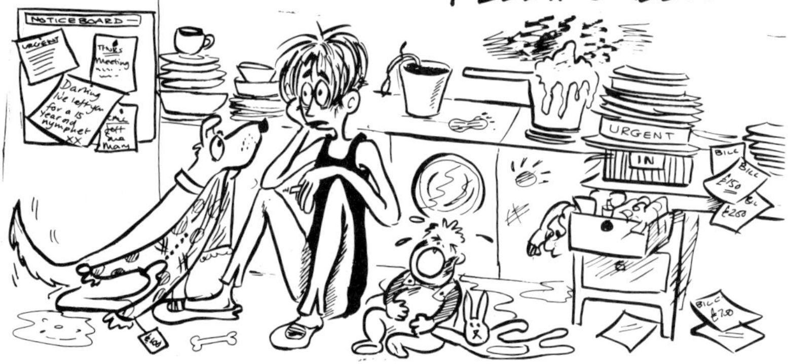

There is a tendency for expressionistic theories of art to claim that a colour's effects are wholly due to its *innate* qualities. Colour is believed to operate almost as an invisible physical force, acting directly on the mind of the observer. The echo, the resonance it sets up, is seen as automatic, inhibited only by a spectator's lack of sensitivity.

Kandinsky conceives of colour as *alive:*

> 'Colour is a power that directly influences the soul. Colour is the keyboard, the eyes are the hammers, the soul is the piano with many strings. The artist is the hand which plays, touching one key or another, to cause vibrations in the soul.'

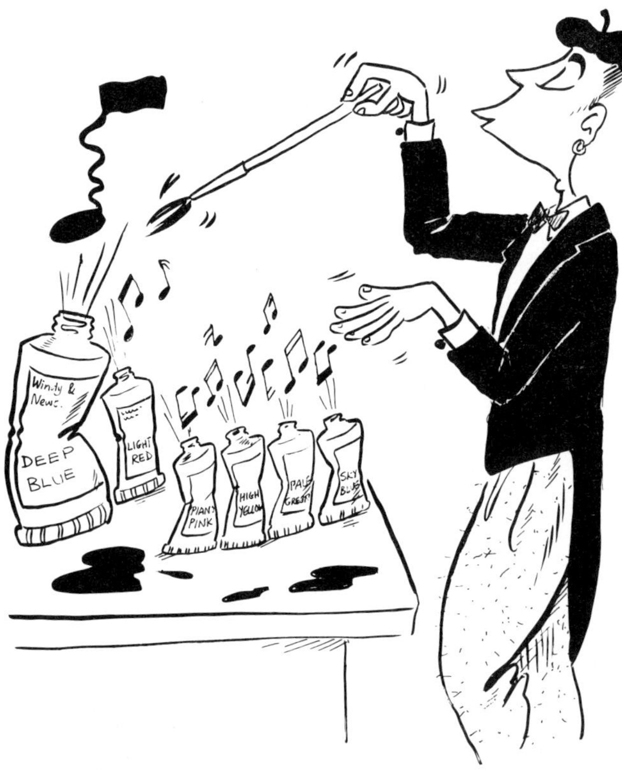

Artists such as Kandinsky believed they were discovering a natural, universal means of expression. Whereas only a Christian could understand an image of a crucifixion, colours and shapes were accessible to everyone.

However, this theoretical perspective ignores the *cultural* dimension which is always present in expression. Different cultures may attach different meanings to the same colour. Furthermore, any given colour may have different meanings even *within* a single culture, depending on the context in which it's found.

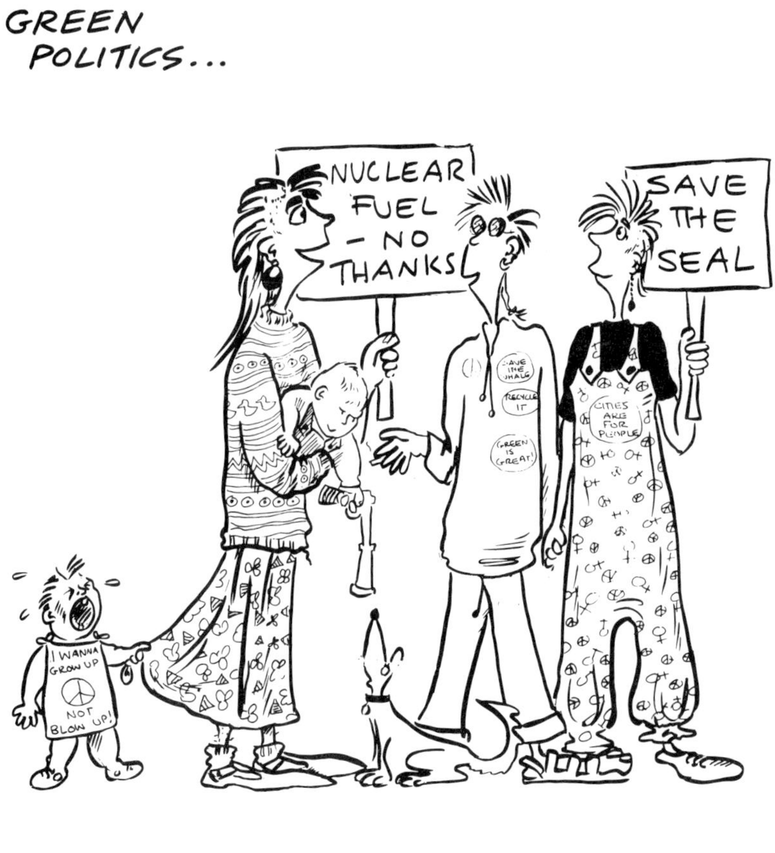

GREEN WITH ENVY...

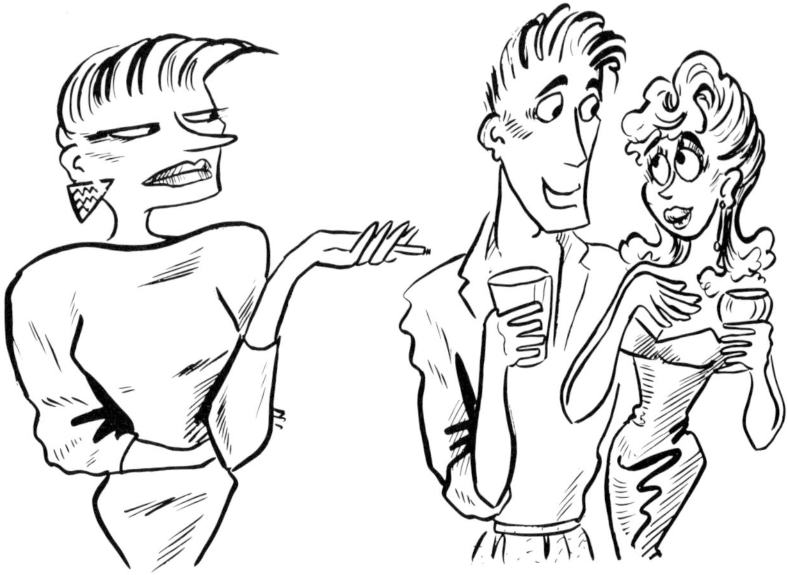

'THIS IS THE NEW BOY– HE'S STILL RATHER GREEN.

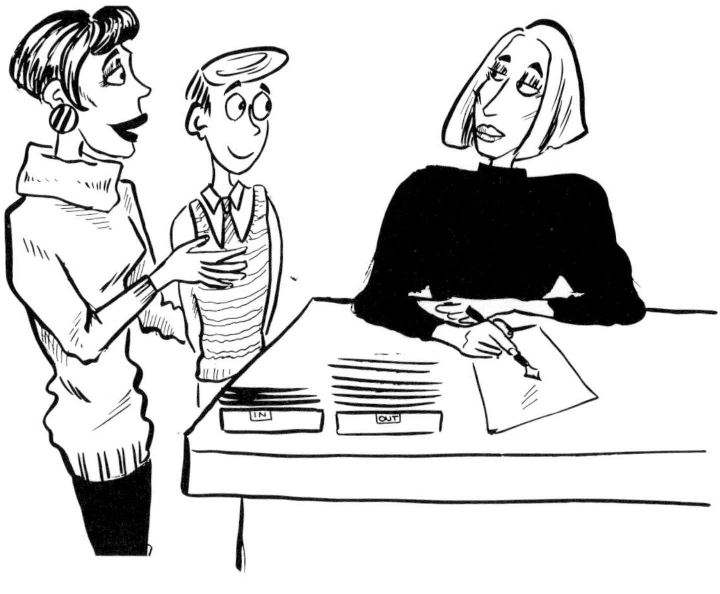

FEELING GREEN...

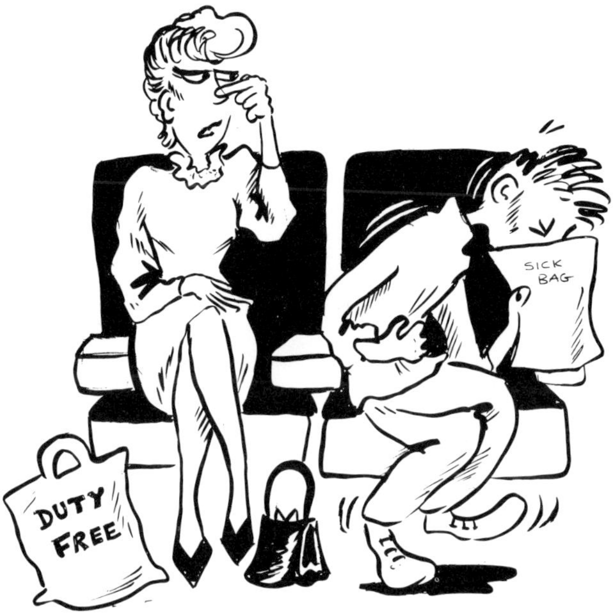

Art is itself one of these contexts, of course. A colour's meaning can vary from one artist to another, and even from one painting to another. For example, a scarlet would read differently in the work of an artist who characteristically painted with a 'hot' palette from another who habitually used only blacks and blues.

Of course, this is not just true of colour. Textures, shape, line and so on are similarly culturally coded. The spectator is not just a passive receiver of stimuli (as in Kandinsky's analogy of the piano) but actively interprets in relation to what he or she already knows. Familiarity with art's codes (which are created within specific cultures) is necessary for meaning to be construed. If communication fails to take place we don't have to make the elitist assumption that the spectator lacks some innate sensitivity (or the philistine one that the artist is a charlatan).

Context

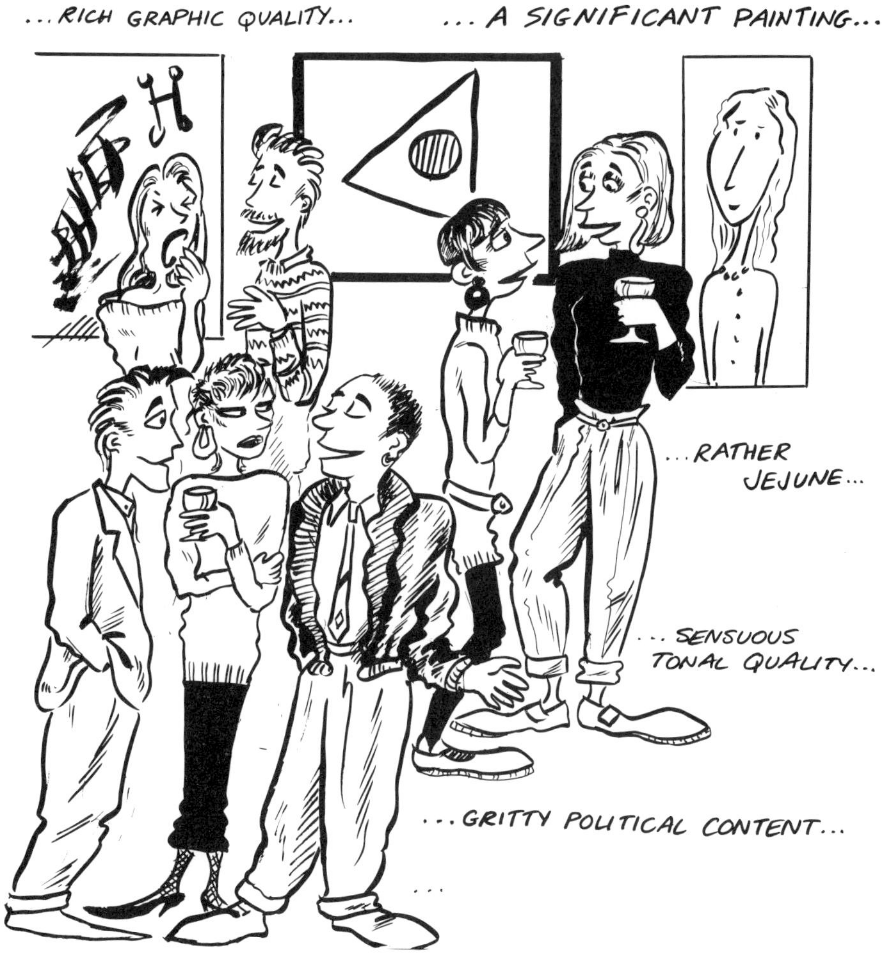
...RICH GRAPHIC QUALITY...
...A SIGNIFICANT PAINTING...
...RATHER JEJUNE...
...SENSUOUS TONAL QUALITY...
...GRITTY POLITICAL CONTENT...
...

As well as thinking about painting and sculpture in contexts specific to art itself, we can extend our understanding by relating them to broader historical and social contexts. For example, Kirchner's *Bathers at Moritzburg* can be placed in the social context of its production. This would mean looking at the very rapid development of the German capitalist economy.

Between 1815 and 1913 employment in German craft and industry nearly trebled, and the value of their output increased ten-fold. The peasantry were transformed into landless 'wage slaves'. By 1910, fifteen times as many Germans lived in cities as had done in 1850.

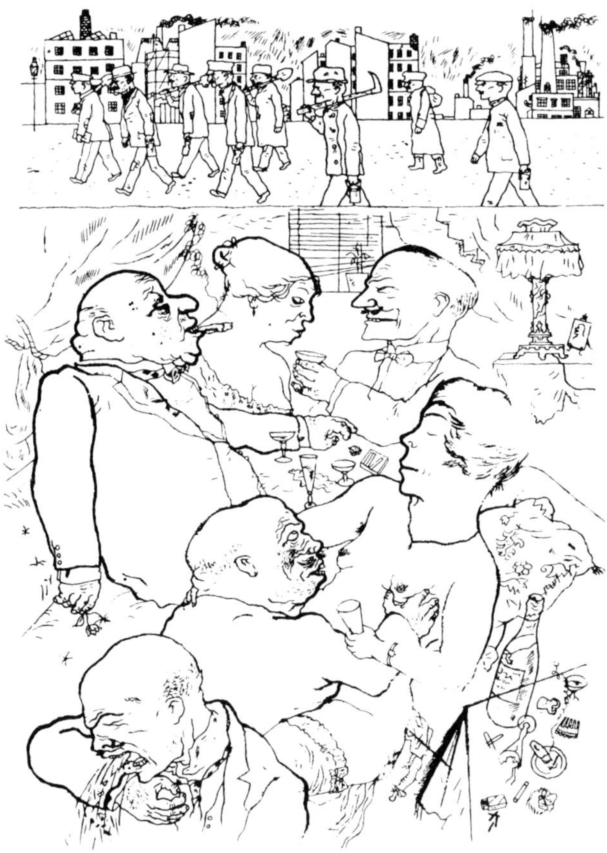

George Grosz *At 5 o'clock in the Morning*

Along with this came:

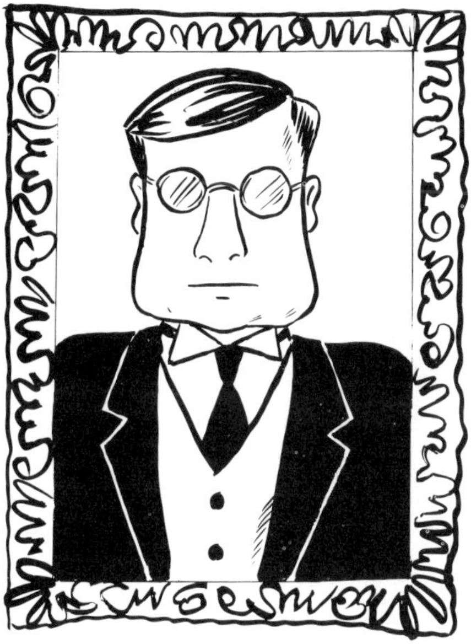

authoritarian government

and militarism

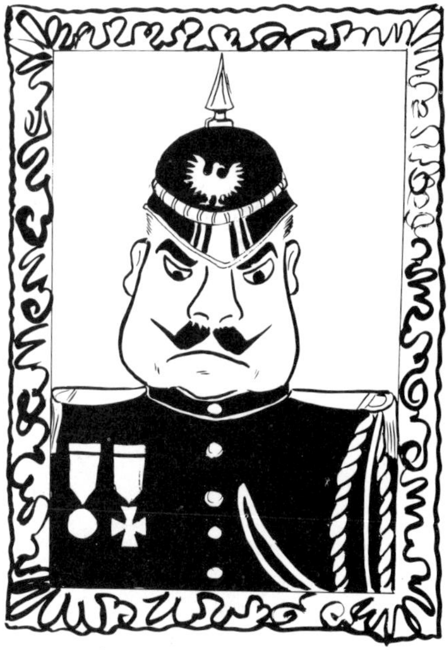

In this materialistic environment, with people cut off from nature, crowded together and working to the mechanical rhythms of the production line creating wealth in which they would not share, it is hardly surprising that feelings of alienation and inauthenticity should arise and find their way into art. The desire for 'self-expression' or 'spontaneity' in painting and sculpture was not just a reaction against the oversophistication and perceived artificiality of the establishment art of the time, but a cry against these same conditions in life itself.

Kirchner's celebration in his painting of nakedness and closeness to nature, as well as the conscious simplicity of its style, needs to be seen against this backdrop and is paralleled by other contemporary phenomena such as the popularity of hiking clubs and the flourishing of the nudist movement.

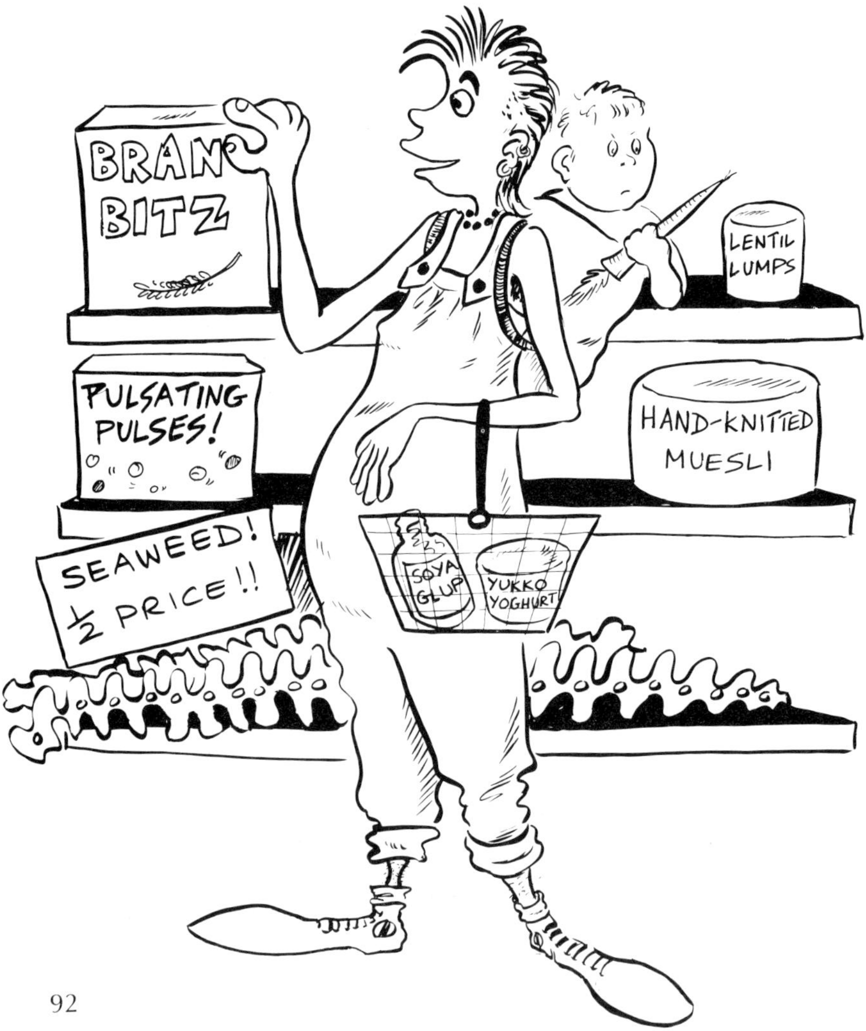

Indeed, the 'back to nature' movement is one that is still with us — whether it is expressed in the desire for holidays in the wilderness, or the popularity of brown bread — and for substantially the same reasons.

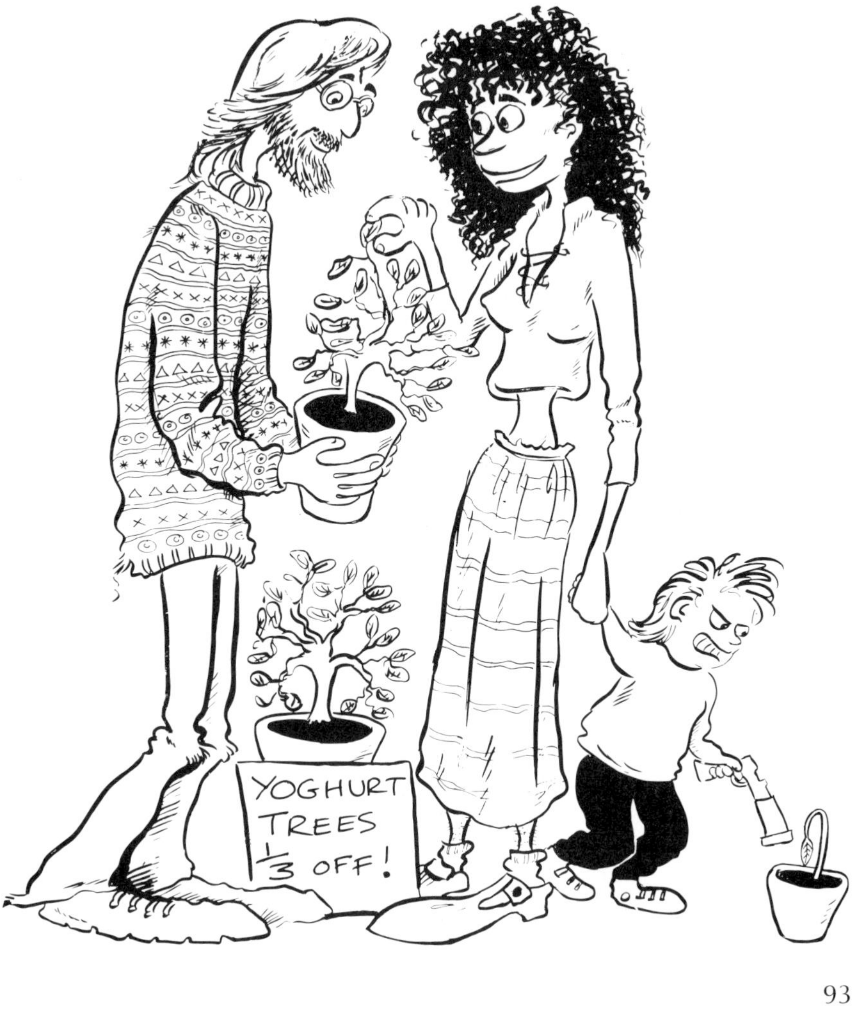

The artificiality and constraints of modern life have led artists, including many of an expressionistic tendency, towards a cult of the 'primitive'. The life of technologically-simpler societies was envied since they were seen as being closer to nature and less problematical for their members.

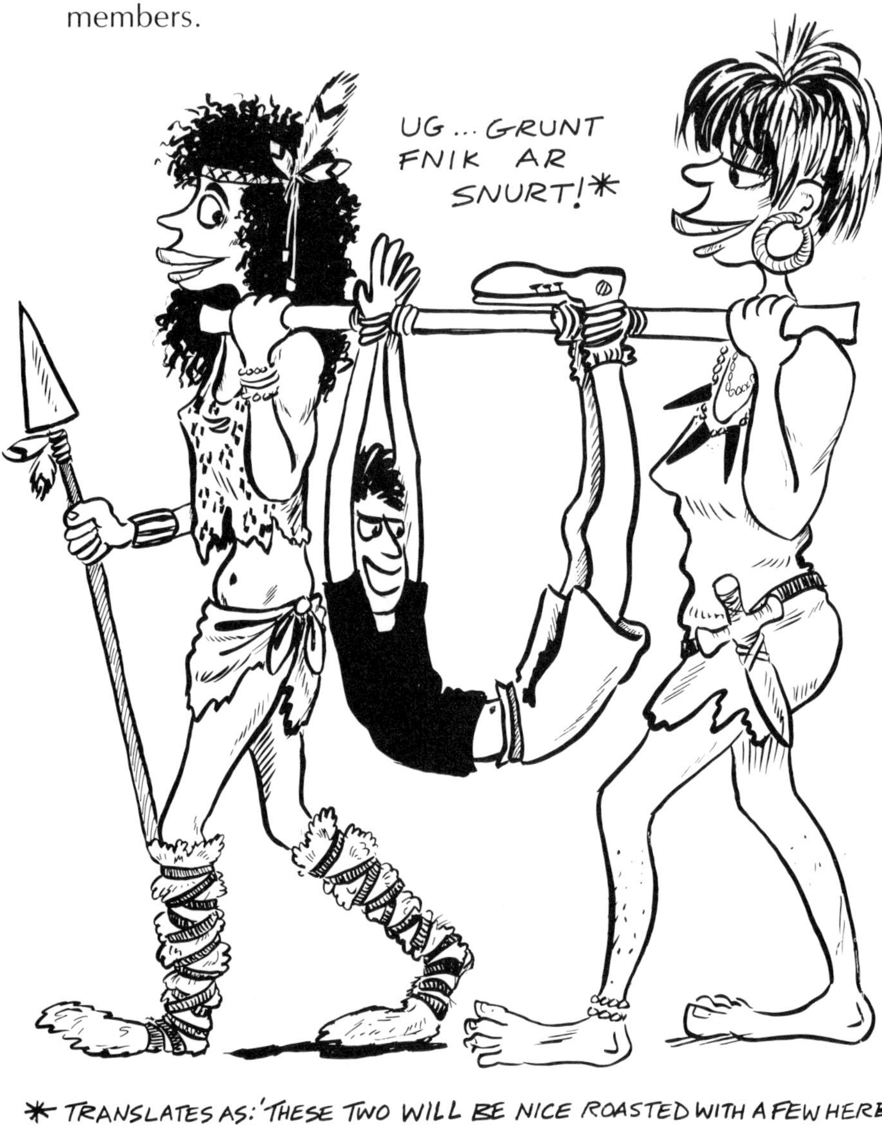

* TRANSLATES AS: 'THESE TWO WILL BE NICE ROASTED WITH A FEW HERBS!'

Some artists actually visited 'primitive' cultures, physically abandoning modern Western life. Paul Gauguin, for example, spent the final years of his life on Tahiti and the Marquesas Islands. For others it was sufficient to seek out stylistic influences from 'primitive' art, or to attempt to cultivate a 'primitive', 'innocent' or 'childlike' state of mind for the act of creation.

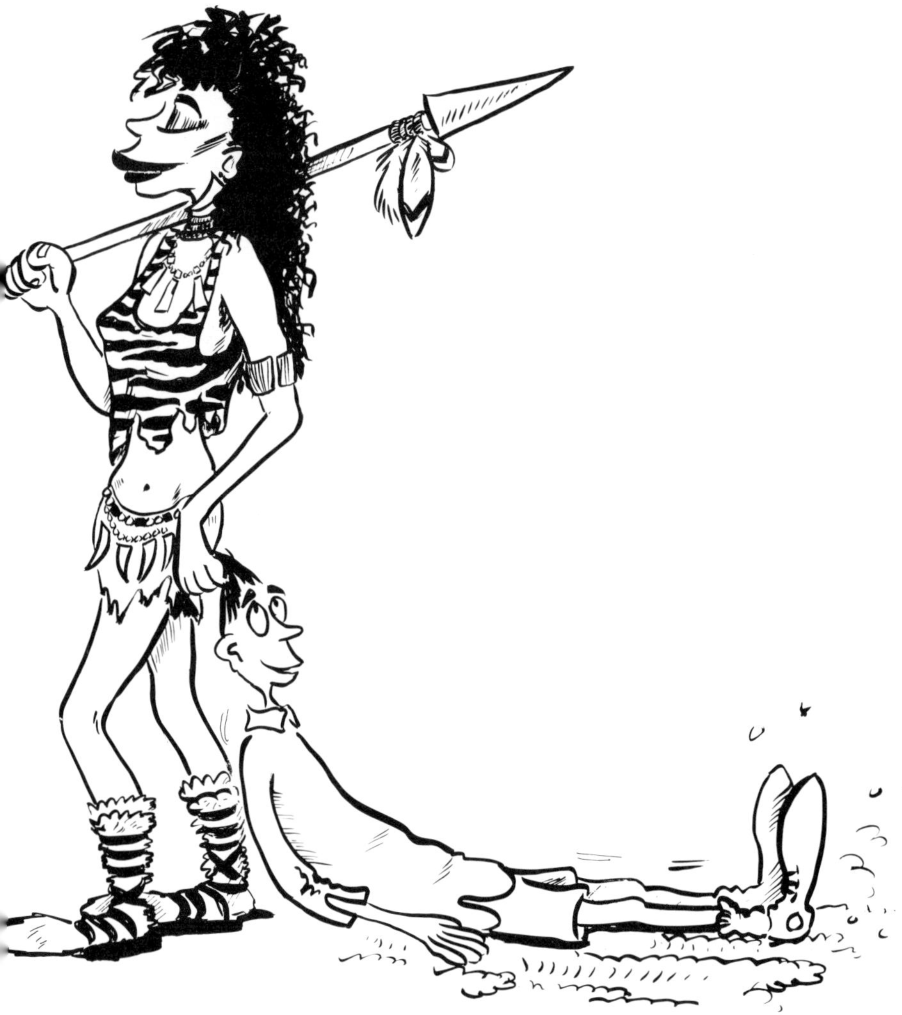

Gauguin's *Arearea (Red Dog)* of 1892, like other works he completed in Tahiti, offers an evocative scene of timeless harmony — something that art has often tried to create.

How we choose to evaluate such paintings will depend on the role we feel art should play. It might be argued that we have a deep-seated need for such comforting images. On the other hand, such escapism *could* be seen as a dangerous abandonment of civilized and rational values.

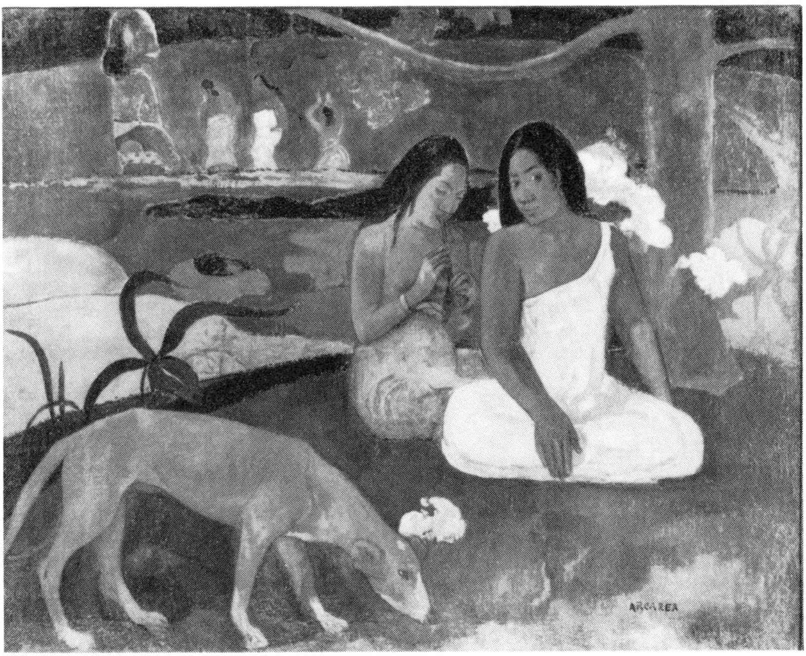

Paul Gauguin *Arearea (Red Dog)* 1892

The 'primitive' alternative could be regarded as *mythical,* not real. Life in small-scale societies is not pre-social — it is governed, like that of our own society, by rules which impose restrictions on the behaviour of its members. What might look from afar like 'closeness to nature' is probably more like poverty from nearer in.

The timeless idyll evoked in *Arearea* is a misrepresentation of historical reality, an abolition of historical analysis by myth. As we said earlier, no image is a neutral 'reflection' of life.

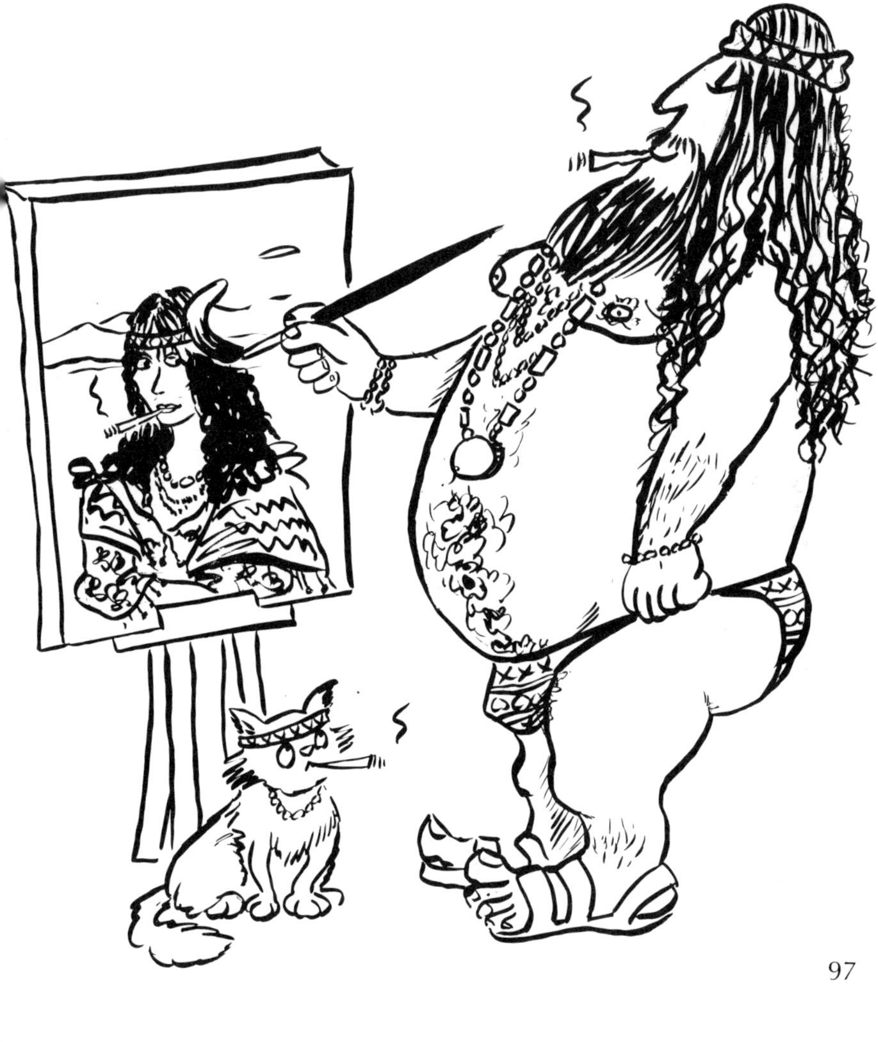

The European colonialists (and the impact of their imperialist expansion on the islands) are consciously edited out of this image. The religious rituals which Gauguin depicts in the background of his painting had in fact long been abandoned because of the destruction of native culture by that same European civilization from which Gauguin had sought to exile himself.

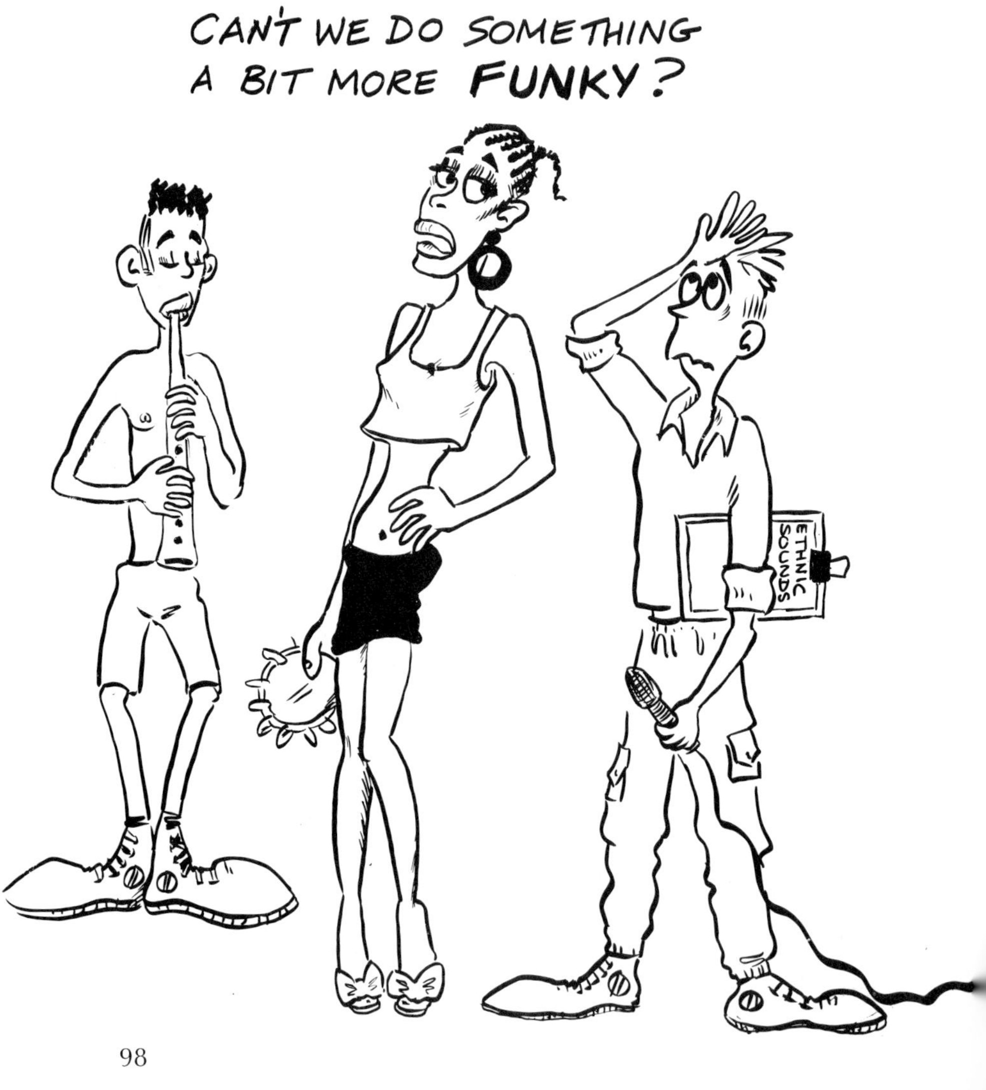

The cult of the 'primitive' (which Gauguin and Kirchner shared) and the interest in 'spontaneity' and 'self expression' that is associated with all expressionistic art are tied up with a particular diagnosis of the problems of the age: an analysis given more in 'spiritual' than material terms. This 'spiritual' diagnosis is shared by many modern artists, including Mondrian and Kandinsky, whose mystical and idealist notions we have already met.

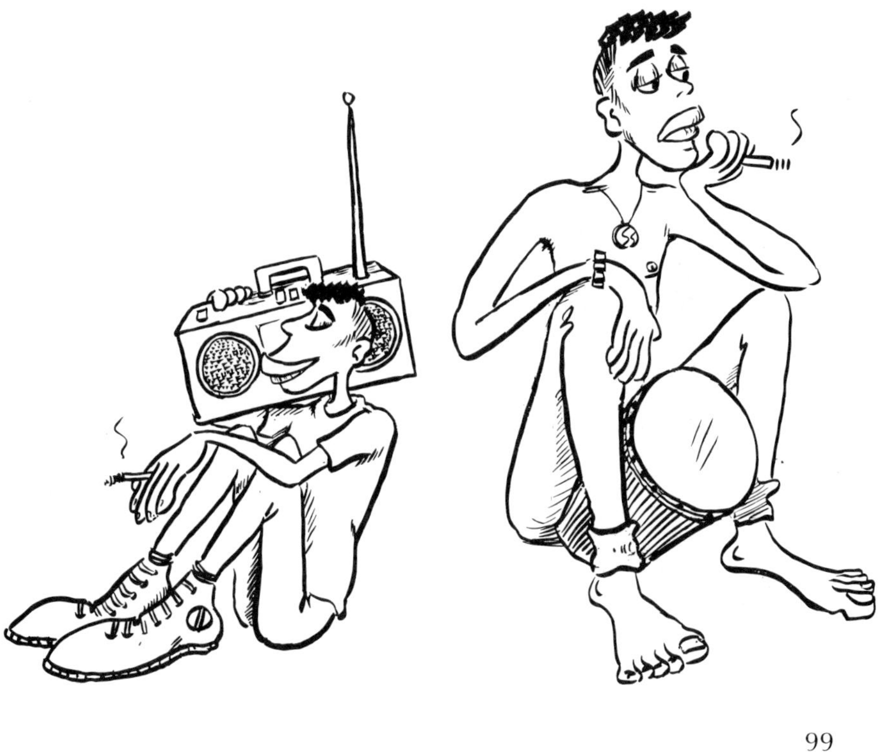

Marx, by contrast, offered a social solution, believing the problems of the time to be rooted in the social and economic realities of capitalist society, with the divorce it created between labour and the wealth that labour produced. For him, the only way forward was to resolve this *material* contradiction by moving towards a socialist society.

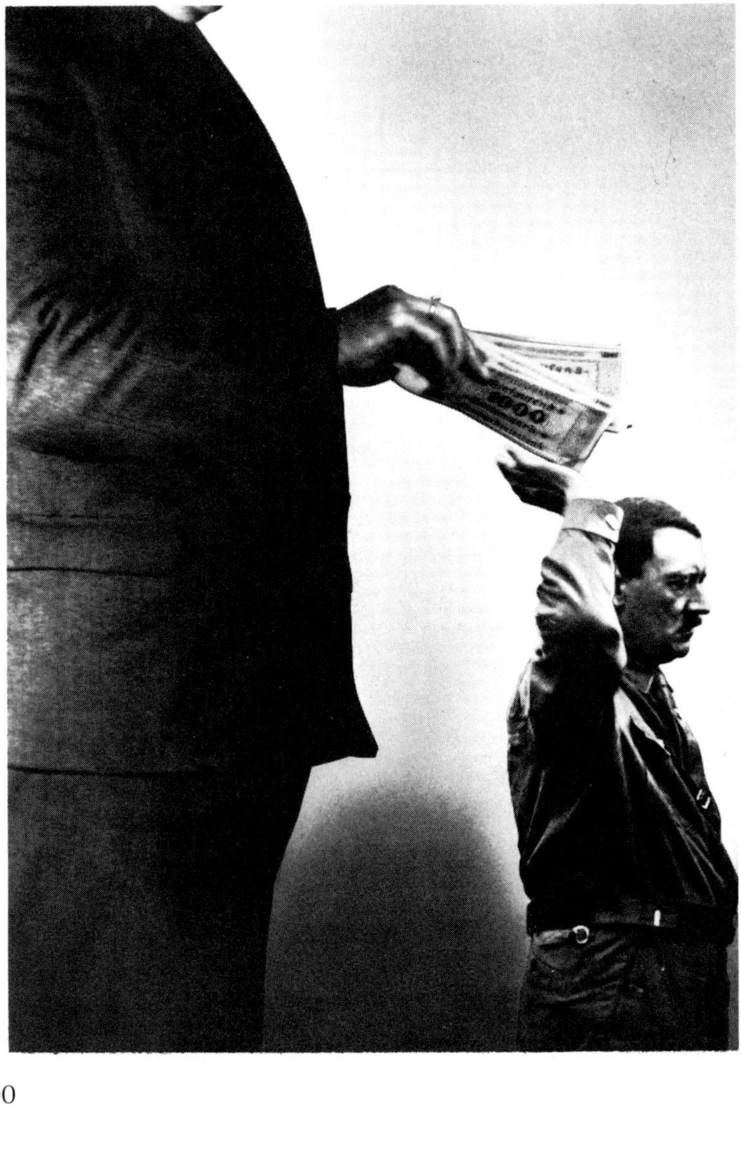

John Heartfield *Millions Stand Behind Me (The Meaning of the Hitler*

This materialist diagnosis of society's ills is embodied in the work of George Grosz and John Heartfield, whose art was concerned to point out the injustices of the age in order to encourage social change.

In Heartfield's photo collage *Millions Stand Behind Me* of 1932, an image of Hitler giving a salute at a Nazi ceremony has been isolated from its original context and juxtaposed with a large and anonymous figure of a capitalist whose financial backing Hitler is thereby shown to receive. The rhetoric of Hitler's salute is subverted, this very same gesture now being made to oppose the Nazi cause. Rather than being a 'big' leader, Hitler becomes a small servant of German capitalism. To represent Nazism as the tool of big business in this way is directly to counter its claims to be a party with mass support, a party of and for the people. Such an image was a daring engagement in German politics in the year before the Nazis came to power.

Modern art, then, is not just one thing; artists have all sorts of ideas about what they are trying to do. Art has served many functions in the modern age and it would be rather undiscerning for someone to like it all. The ability to respond to art is learnt, it's not just something that some people have and other haven't. And the role of the spectator is not a passive one. It's not just a case of having 'sensitive feelings' in front of a work of art. How we evaluate a painting or sculpture will depend on a host of extra-artistic matters, including our political and spiritual beliefs. We have to make choices. Should art concern itself with 'absolutes', or with contemporary social reality?

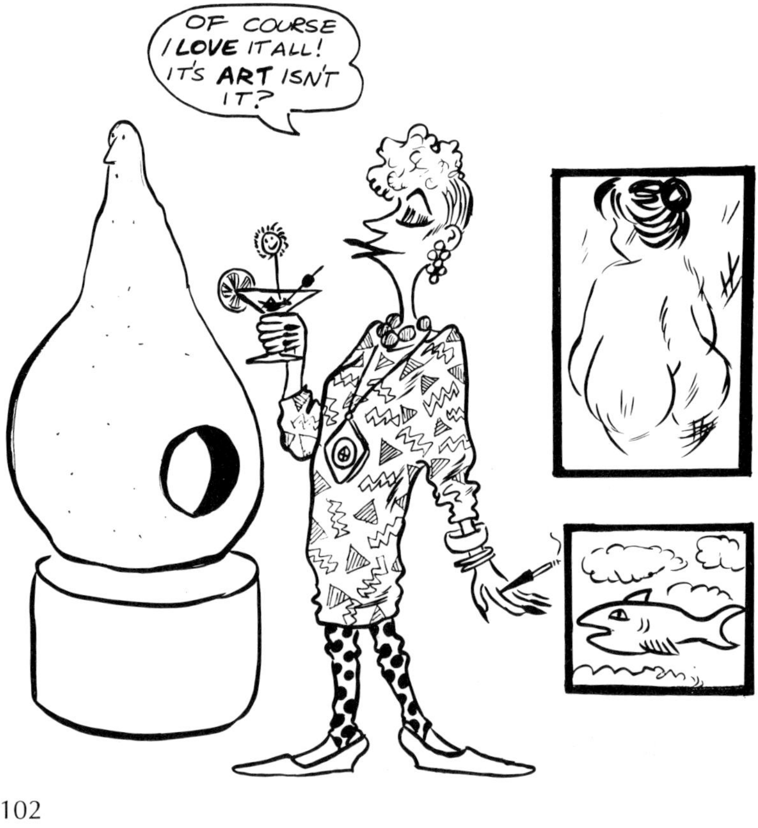

It is frequently suggested that we should approach art with an open, innocent mind. Not only is this impossible but the attempt to do so is undesirable. Our ideas and experience of life must be brought to the viewing of art if we are to *make* sense of it in a discriminating way. And in the case of good art those ideas and experiences may be transformed in the process.

If this way of responding to art sounds too cerebral (especially after our discussion of Expressionism) then we should remind ourselves that emotions will be part of the experience of life we bring to art, and they too can be reordered by it.

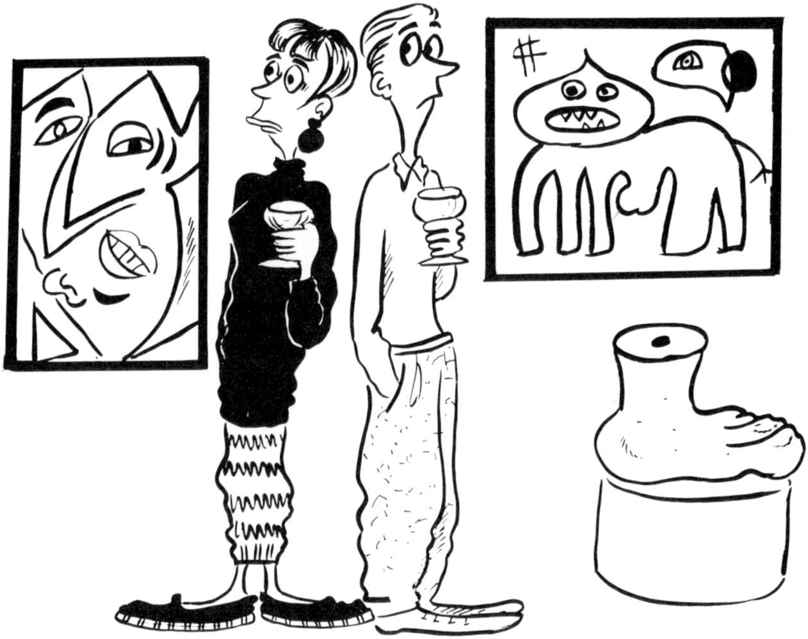

All representation involves classification. Like descriptive art, expressive art embodies decisions about what it is important to show — in this case it pinpoints *feelings.* In selecting from the range of possible emotions, expressive art does not merely evoke feelings so that the spectator can wallow in them; it places emotions in a context. Art has something to assert about them.

Modern art is sometimes charged with being elitist — with being a cultural property exclusive to the powerful few. But this has been true of all art.

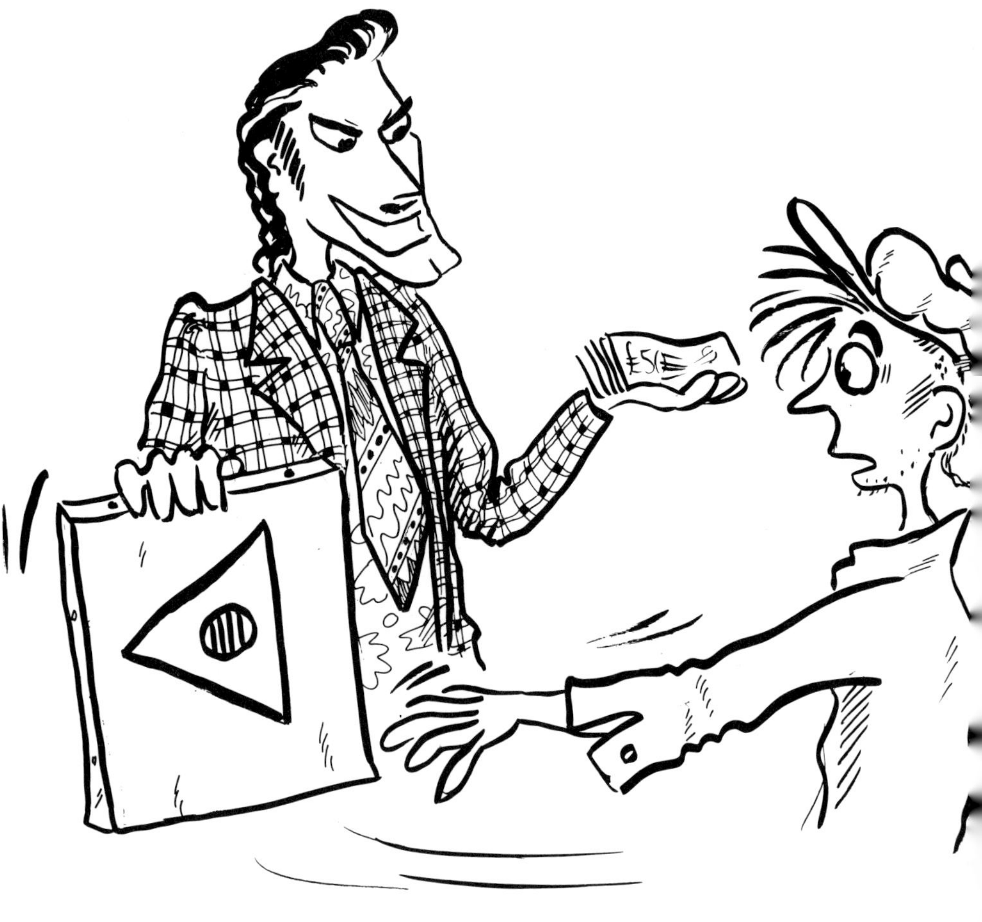

Art has always belonged to someone, whether this someone was a member of the Medici family of Renaissance Florence.

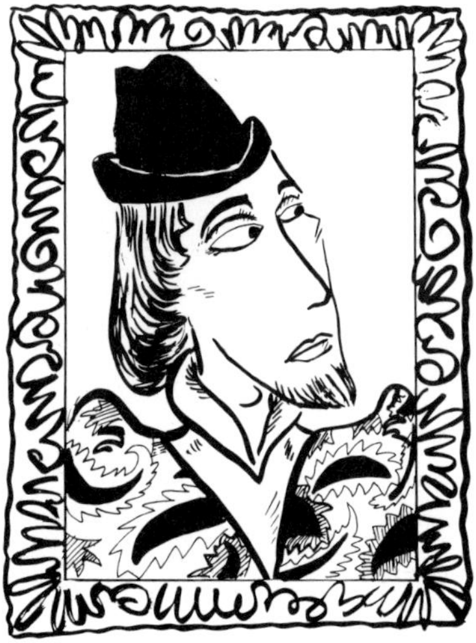

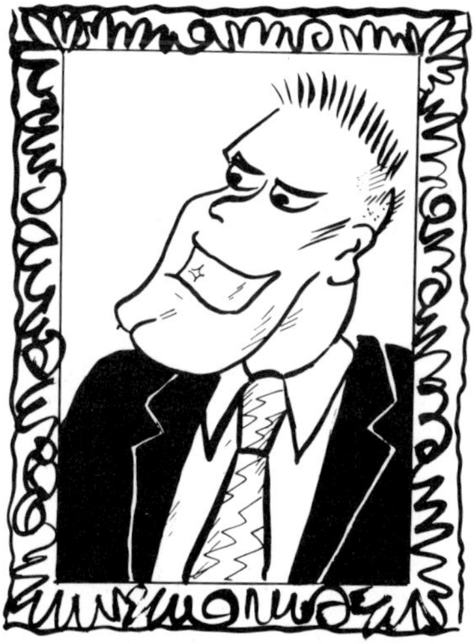

Or the Rockefeller family of 20th century USA.

Not only have individual art objects belonged to particular patrons who bought or commissioned them to display their power and wealth, but the most prominent art of any age has also tended to 'belong' in a broader sense to the dominant class or interest group. Those who have the economic power (because they own the means of production) tend to have the political power too. And also the *cultural* power.

Art always embodies the values, perspectives, and interests of its paymasters. What art is allowed to say, and what types of art survive, depends in some degree on who has the power in society at any one time. In this sense, then, all art is political.

The many paintings of racehorses, hunting scenes, and country houses in 18th century English art (George Stubbs is only the tip of an iceberg) are a consequence of the continuing power of the landed classes. They show the particular recreational pursuits favoured by the gentry and aristocracy and the possessions they valued.

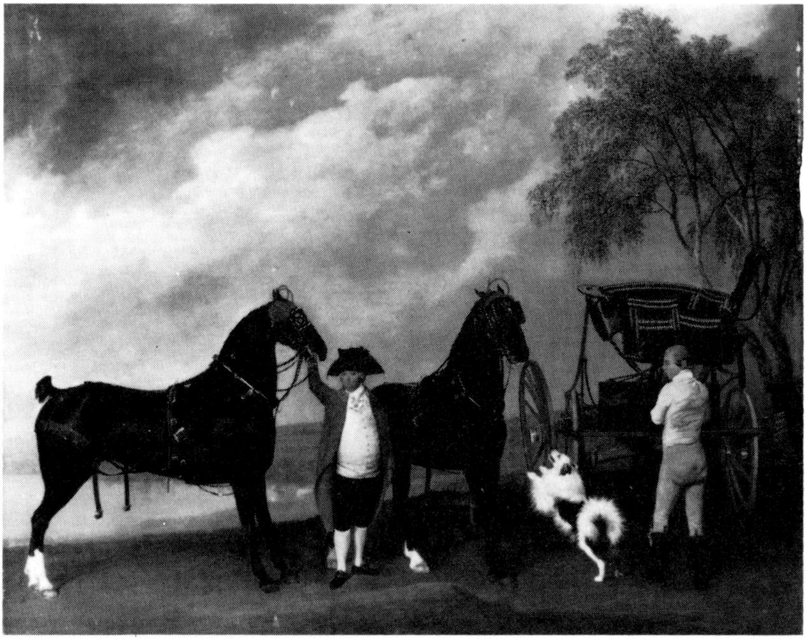

George Stubbs *The Prince of Wales' Phaeton* 1793

Since the Industrial Revolution, economic and social power has transferred largely to the bourgeoisie, and this has meant a great expansion in the patronage of art. Impressionist artists such as Monet, Berthe Morisot and Auguste Renoir benefited from this — the smaller canvases they produced were more suitable for private houses than the large ones produced by other French artists with a state purchase in mind. Whereas Stubbs represents the rural environment which provided the agricultural power base of his patrons, most Impressionists concentrated on the fashionable forms of urban and suburban middle-class existence, particularly the new leisure activities. Scenes of working class life are uncommon, and work is almost never shown in their selective images of the modern world.

It is not just in choices about *what* is represented that the perspective of the powerful finds its way into art, but also in decisions about *how* something is shown. Gauguin's Tahitian paintings may not represent the world of the European middle classes but it is *their* Tahiti that is shown, not that of the islanders themselves.

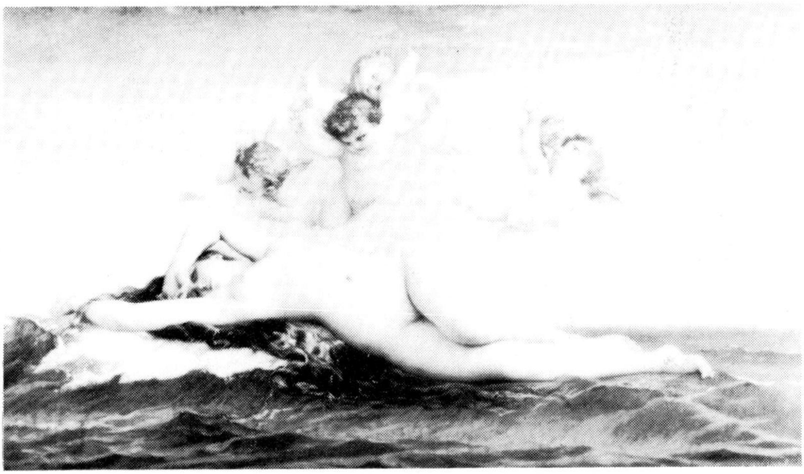
Alexander Cabanel *Birth of Venus* 1863

Power relations of gender as well as those of class and empire are also expressed and legitimized in art. Cabanel's *Birth of the Venus* may show a woman, but clearly it was painted with *male* purchasing power in mind. By her reclining pose, this so-called 'Venus' places the spectator in a dominant, possessive role, and in the way her body is revealed to our gaze she is reduced to an object for (male) erotic interest.

Institutions of art education are one channel through which the interests of the dominant social group become established in art. Schools and academies are able to determine who gets the necessary technical training and thus can control entry to the profession. (The relatively small number of women artists in history is partly explained by the difficulties they have experienced in gaining professional status).

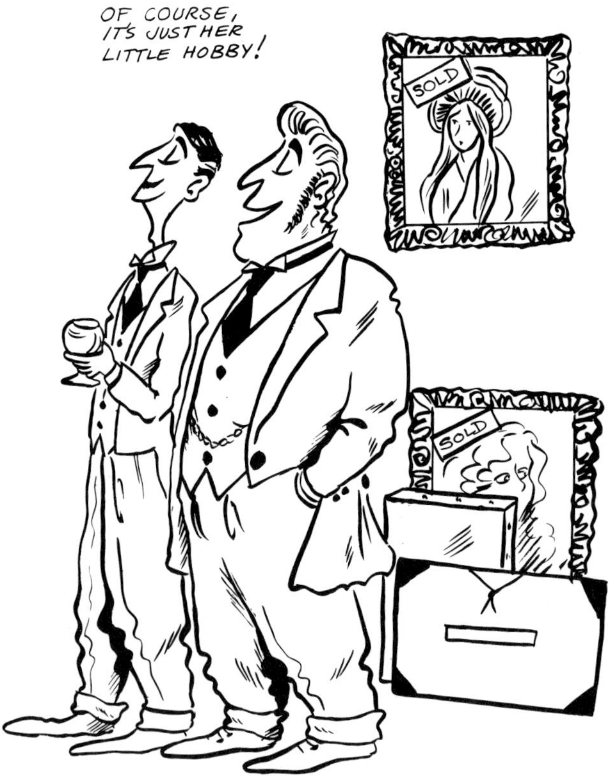

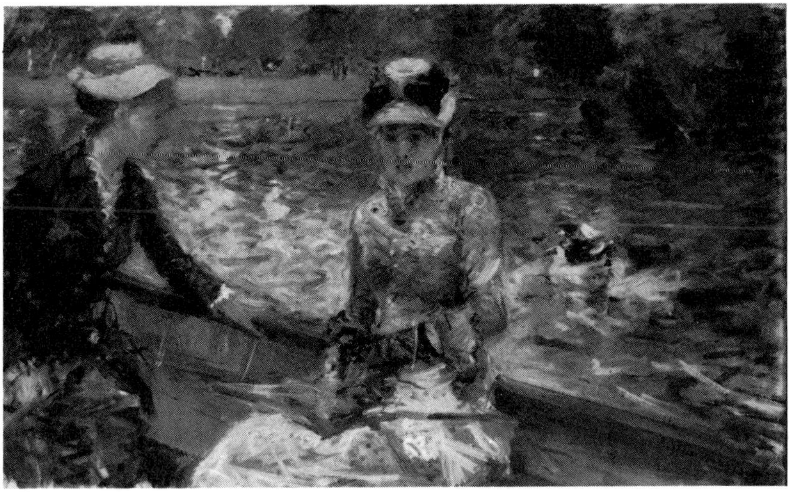

Berthe Morisot *Summer Day* 1879

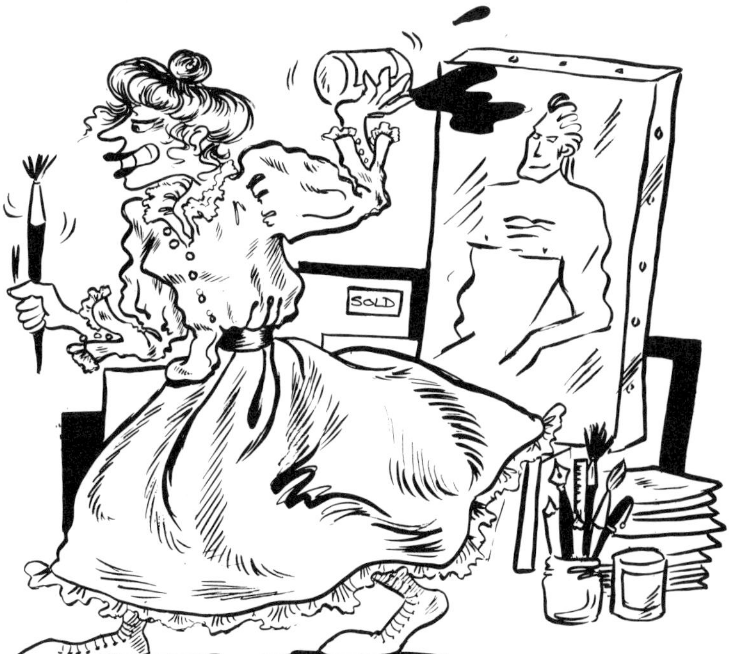

But the key means by which economic power becomes cultural power is through patronage. The modern period has seen important changes in the institutions of the art market.

In early 19th century France, the royal Salons provided virtually the only opportunity for artists to display and sell new work. Entry to these Salons were controlled by a jury nominated by the political establishment and by established artists. Consequently, it tended to reject politically or artistically radical work.

To escape the virtual monopoly of the state-run Salon and find an alternative outlet for the sale of their paintings, from 1874 the Impressionists held private exhibitions of their own. Soon they and all artists that followed them were able to benefit from the rise of the system of private art dealers which emerged to cater for the expanding demands of middle class patrons. Novelty, which had previously been penalised, now became a virtue since it enabled your goods to stand out from the others on display in the marketplace.

The agreement Picasso made with his dealer Kahnweiler in 1912 was similar to the contracts many other artists have subsequently entered into. The dealer promised to buy all of Picasso's current output, the price being determined in advance relative to the size of the canvas (not with respect to any notion of how good the work was).

For those artists favoured with such contracts the obvious advantage was the freedom it gave them from having to please Salon juries or the public at large. They had a guaranteed income (and in Picasso's case a good one), though we must remember that this freedom was limited by the market. In the long term, artists had to produce work that would sell or dealers would not renew their contracts and they would lose their place in the shop

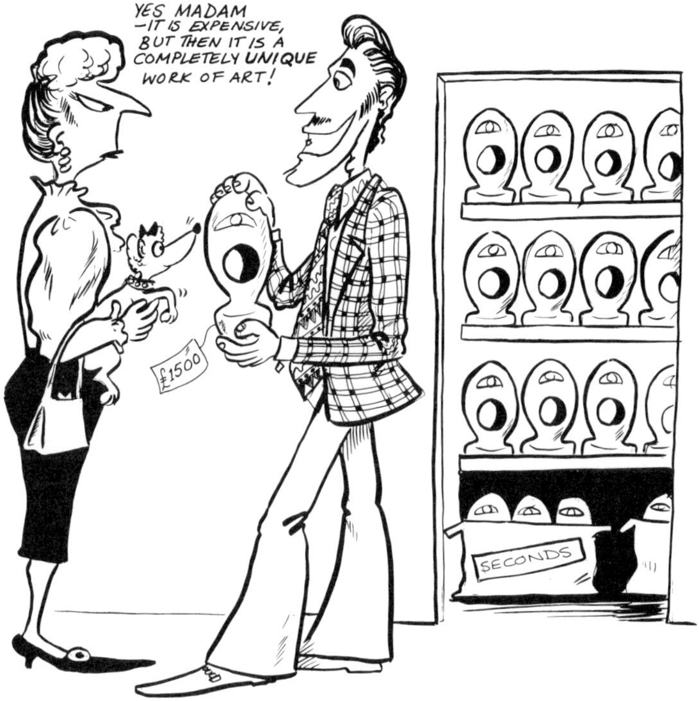

window. Most dealers, then and now, expect to sell works for a mark up of around 100% on the money they have paid to the artist. In the case of Picasso's Cubist paintings, only a few rich patrons were buying, and Kahnweiler's strategy was to hold on to the bulk of his Picassos in the hope that prices would rise — his monopoly giving him complete control over the supply of new paintings to the market.

Speculation in works of art is commonplace — artists, dealers and collectors all share a vested interest in the promotion of a reputation. The hand-made nature of paintings and sculptures provides a convenient guarantee of their relative scarcity as commodities. Modern art is

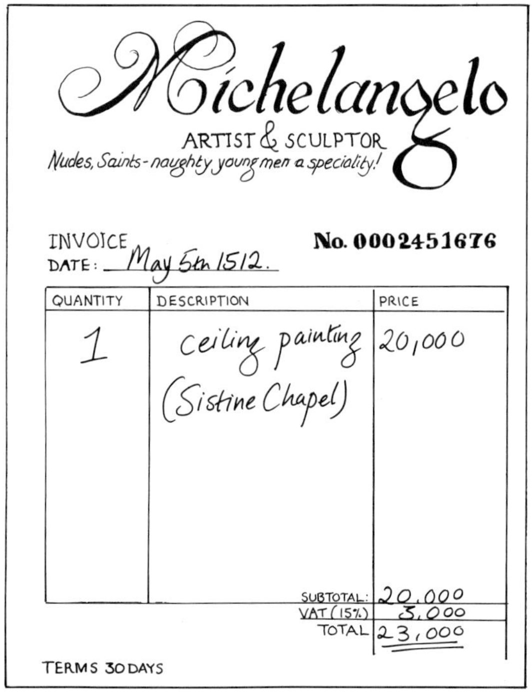

Michelangelo
ARTIST & SCULPTOR
Nudes, Saints - naughty young men a speciality!

INVOICE
DATE: May 5th 1512.
No. 0002451676

QUANTITY	DESCRIPTION	PRICE
1	ceiling painting (Sistine Chapel)	20,000
	SUBTOTAL:	20,000
	VAT (15%)	3,000
	TOTAL	23,000

TERMS 30 DAYS

especially suitable for speculative investment. Not many Rembrandts come onto the market and his reputation is a stable one — he is hardly waiting to be discovered. Modern artists' work can be bought more cheaply with the hope of selling at a profit if prices rise.

Art tends to be talked about as the product of isolated geniuses, and many modern artists have been only too willing to encourage this image of the painter as a seer or prophet, standing outside of society and its demands. But even if this view isn't very helpful in trying to understand art, nor is its opposite.

'They only do it for the money' is a statement usually reserved for artists we don't wish to take seriously. But of course on one level every painting or sculpture is a product for the market place, a commodity like any other. The artist is a producer, and it is not necessarily a denigration of anyone's creative powers to acknowledge the fact — it applies as much to Michelangelo as it does to the most commercially-minded charlatan.

Let me emphasize: I am not saying that art is 'nothing but' the outcome of the economic and social forces that are at work on it. If this were so, art would be of little interest.

Such forces are a real determinant of art (not a mere 'background' to it), but art has a *relative autonomy* from economic and social realities — it is not just a direct 'reflection' of social life. It is in this relative autonomy (which can vary in degree) that the power of art to make a useful contribution to our knowledge of the world lies.

This conditional freedom of art gives it the potential to make critical statements about the society in which it was created; to stand outside the dominant values of that society and to take an oppositional role. Society certainly shapes art, but art also has a role in shaping society. Artistic representations can either provide one of the means by which the status quo is reinforced (or perhaps we should say 'reproduced', since society is constantly being remade, if only in its own image). Or they can provide one of the means by which to challenge and alter existing conditions. One group of modern artists who have attempted this latter task are the Surrealists.

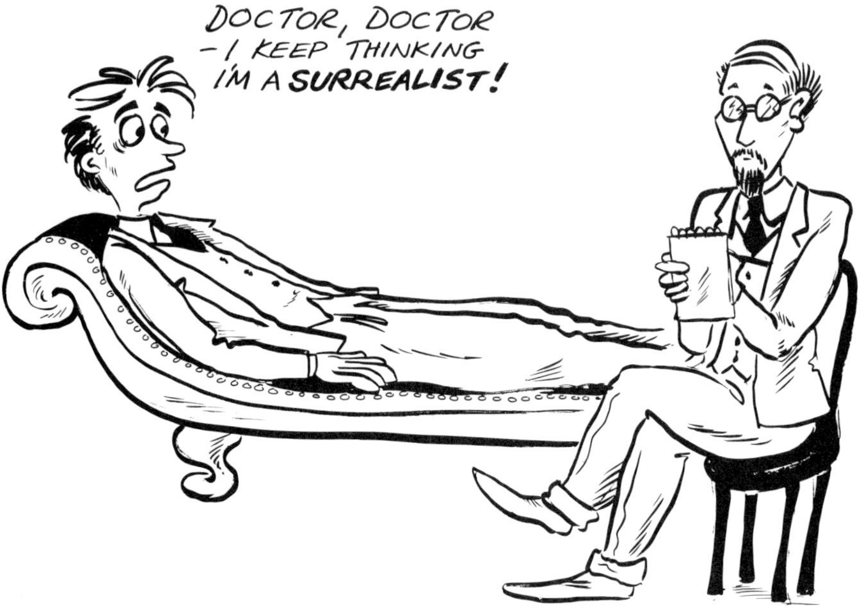

The Surrealists (who include artists such as Joan Mirò, Max Ernst, René Magritte and Salvador Dali) are sometimes seen as 'fantasy' painters. Like many modern artists they were motivated by the desire to explore the inner world of the mind, not just visible reality. Unlike most other artists, though, they conceived this search in materialist terms. Drawing on the writings of Freud and his notion of the 'unconscious', their thinking was psychological rather than spiritual in character. Like Freud, they felt that there were many forces in the mind not controlled by our rational conscious awareness.

Despite what is commonly thought, the Surrealists did not merely abandon themselves to irrationality, but attempted to use this territory of the unconscious mind to help criticize current notions of what 'rationality' meant. For example, the horrors of the First World War were seen as the direct result of this so-called 'civilized', 'rational' mentality, and a more expanded idea of the rational was sought. Art was one weapon in the Surrealists' attack on 'bourgeois' ideas of 'rationality'.

For the Surrealists there was the particular hope that art would release from the unconscious desires that had been repressed by current society — desires with a subversive potential. An energy was to be liberated that would fuel a revolt against the oppressive structures of present day civilization that had been embodied even in the individual psyche.

Art was felt to provide a sheltered arena in which unconscious contents could surface into the light of day and be reconciled with the conscious mind.

According to Freud, dream was an area in which unconscious conflicts and repressed desires could express themselves, and some Surrealist art, such as Dali's, tries to evoke the mood of dreams. The cryptic symbols that occur in dreams are parallel to the metaphoric language

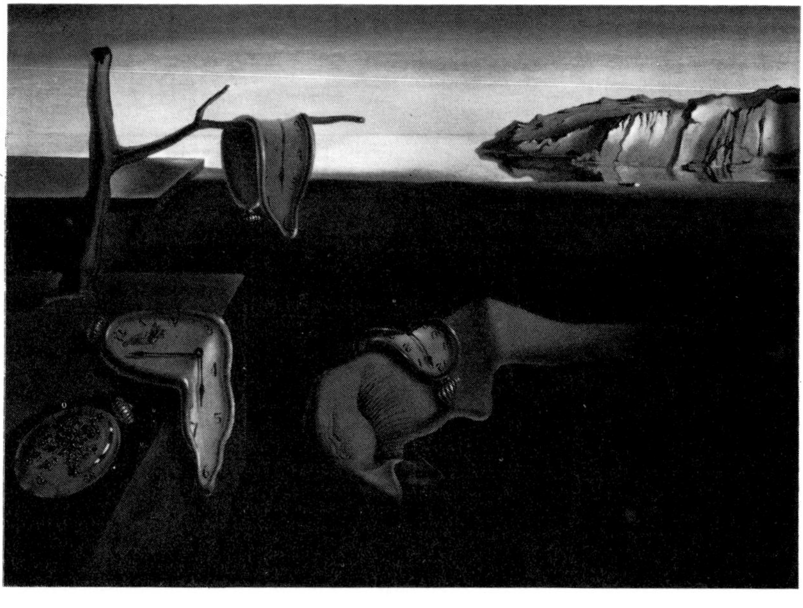

Salvador Dali *The Persistence of Memory* 1931

of some art, and the 'unwilled' quality of dream imagery has similarities to the partly-intuitive nature of this artistic symbolism.

The symbolic language of Mirò's art allows him to deal with sexual themes which socially imposed taboos would make it difficult to 'discuss' in a more 'realistic' style, rather as dreams use a roundabout idiom to veil a comparable content.

This parallel between dream and art must not be pushed too far. Art can provide a framed-off area where the imaginative life is given more rein than in normal activity, but pure fantasy does have to make some

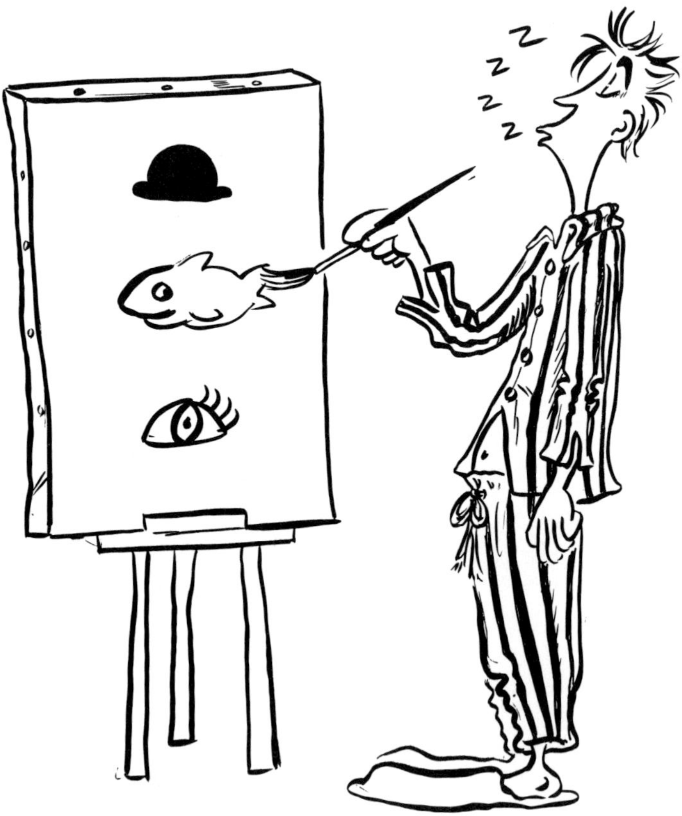

compromises with reality if it is to be transformed into art. For instance, painting technique itself demands the intrusion of conscious effort.

Art, then, provides a half way stage between dream and 'real' life, serving a function in adult life similar to the one which play performs in childhood. Play with a toy doll, say, represents a stepping stone between the infant's incorporation of external reality into its fantasy life and its full acknowledgement of the separate existence of other individuals. In play, as in art, utilitarian goals are held in abeyance. Play may *ultimately* be useful, but only so long as it is not required to be serious and purposeful.

When unconscious fantasy erupts into art, it does so only selectively, and through the shared, public conventions of artistic language. In this it is no different from art with an expressive or descriptive content.

With their interest in the 'as if' world of fantasy, the Surrealists found the new styles developed by modern artists especially useful. The innovations of artists such as Picasso were plundered, their formal vocabularies adapted for new uses.

In the protected domain of art, novel 'mutations' of thought could be thrown up, prototypes tried out, and imaginative leaps made that could not yet be sustained in life at large. One common strategy in Surrealist art is to bring diverse objects together in unlikely juxtapositions which parallel the bizarre happenings of dreams.

Although the unconscious may find associations that link the objects, and invest them with a symbolic resonance, the rational mind fails to explain away the encounter. The result is that we experience a sense of estrangement from what we had previously regarded as familiar reality. Outside of their normal context of use, objects are endowed with a novel poetry, and a sense of wonder is restored to our relations with the world. The

Surrealist desire is that this unsettling of our 'ordinary' mentality might loosen the bonds of our social conditioning.

Max Ernst's technique of bringing together widely differing fragments of reality can be disturbing or hallucinatory, but there is often some kind of humorous potential present too.

Ernst often relies on the collage method (as here), which provides an ideal means of creating unfamiliar juxtapositions. The ready-made images that he uses were plundered from the engravings in commercial catalogues, popular fiction and encyclopaedias of the late 19th century. By appropriating a visual imagery deeply imbued with the values of bourgeois society, Ernst's aim is to subvert that society with its own productions. Dominant but hidden codes and conventions are exposed — and exposed to ridicule.

When Magritte and Dali create painted equivalents to Ernst's collages, they do so not in a 'modern' but in an illusionistic style. The chance to use a society's favoured style against that society must have seemed too good to miss.

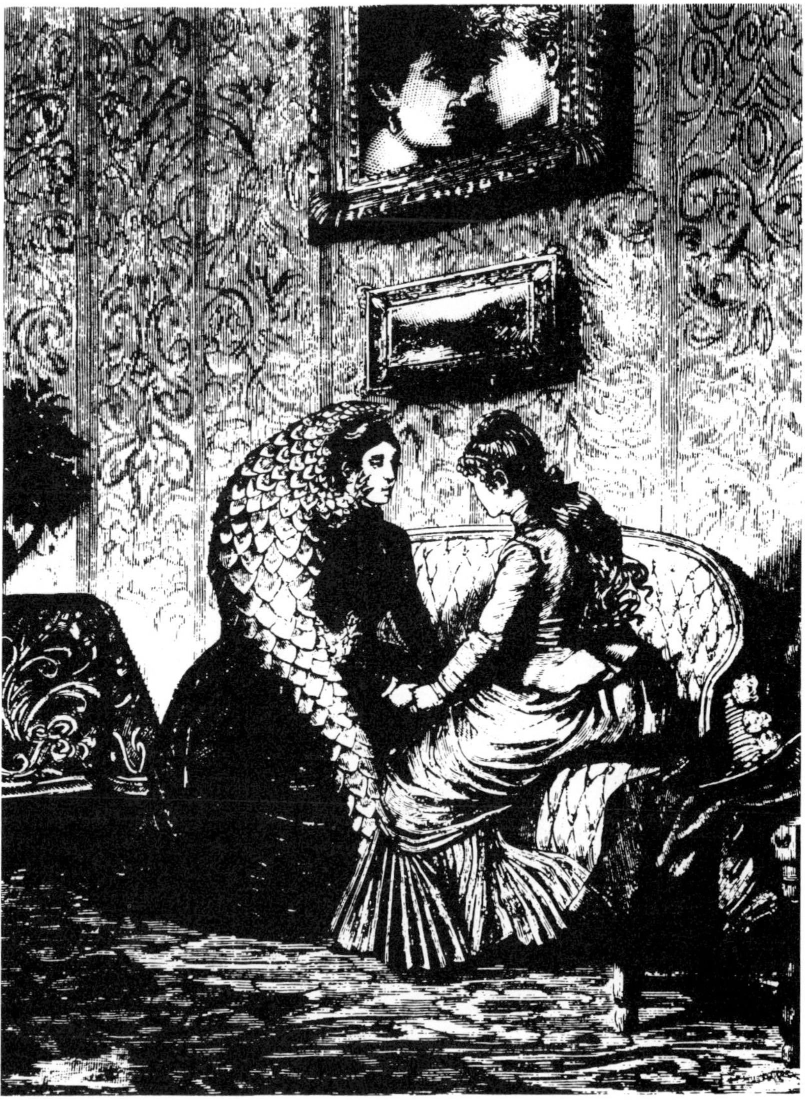

Max Ernst plate from collage novel A *Week of Plenty*

The Surrealists are sometimes accused of using art for a non-artistic purpose, but perhaps *all* good art challenges us to see the world in a new way. Certainly Edouard Manet (considered by many to be the first 'modern' artist) can be seen to have adopted a similarly critical attitude to prevailing visual culture.

In *Olympia* of 1865, he attempts to comment on and subvert the conventions we have observed in paintings such as Cabanel's *Birth of Venus*.

In *The Birth of Venus* an ostensibly mythological theme helps disguise the fact that the work is essentially a piece of pornography. Manet's *Olympia* also adopts a classical reference in the title, but since the young woman who is its subject is most obviously *not* a goddess, a disjunction is created. Once Manet's parody of the convention has brought it to our attention, we are able to transfer our insight back onto paintings such as Cabanel's, thereby demystifying them.

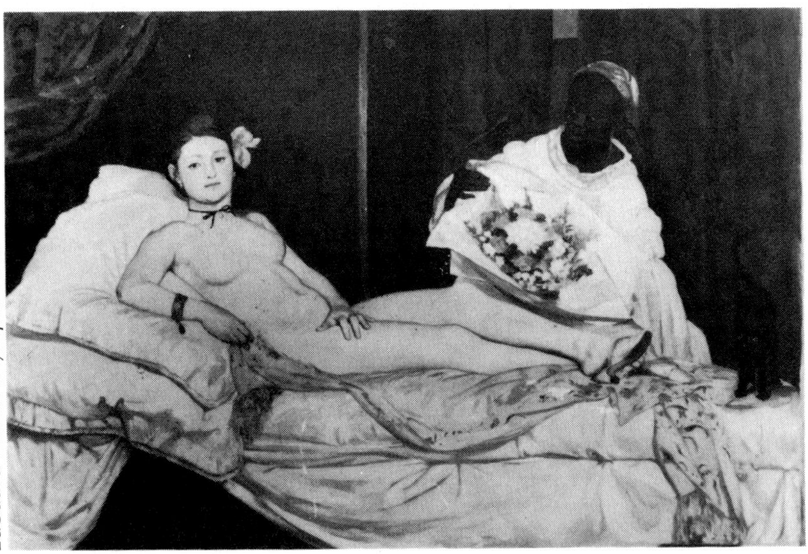

Edouard Manet *Olympia* 1865

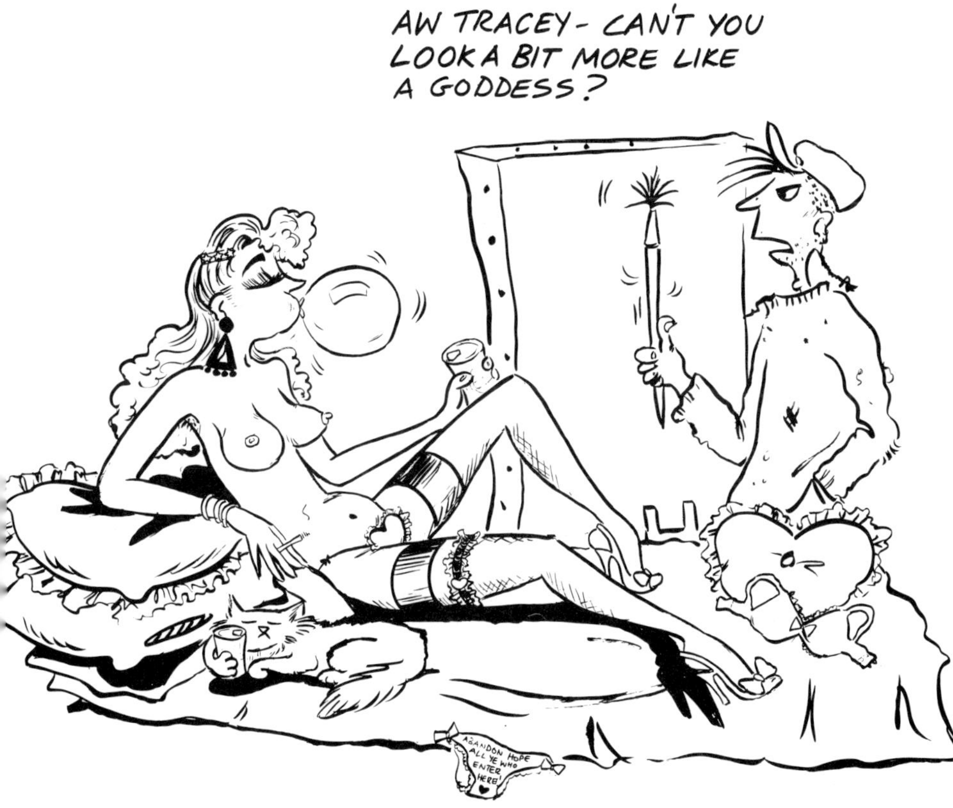

Whereas Cabanel shows us a timeless, idealized vision of Woman, Manet is at pains to present a particularized, contemporary image of *a* woman — even specifying her social class. Whereas Cabanel represents woman as the object of male desire, Manet points us to a social context — prostitution, which provided a common source of income for single women alone in Paris. A parallel is evident between the way women are treated in life and the way they are represented in art. Manet underlines this by situating the spectator as the newly-arrived client whose bouquet of flowers is being presented (and whom the cat so evidently dislikes!).

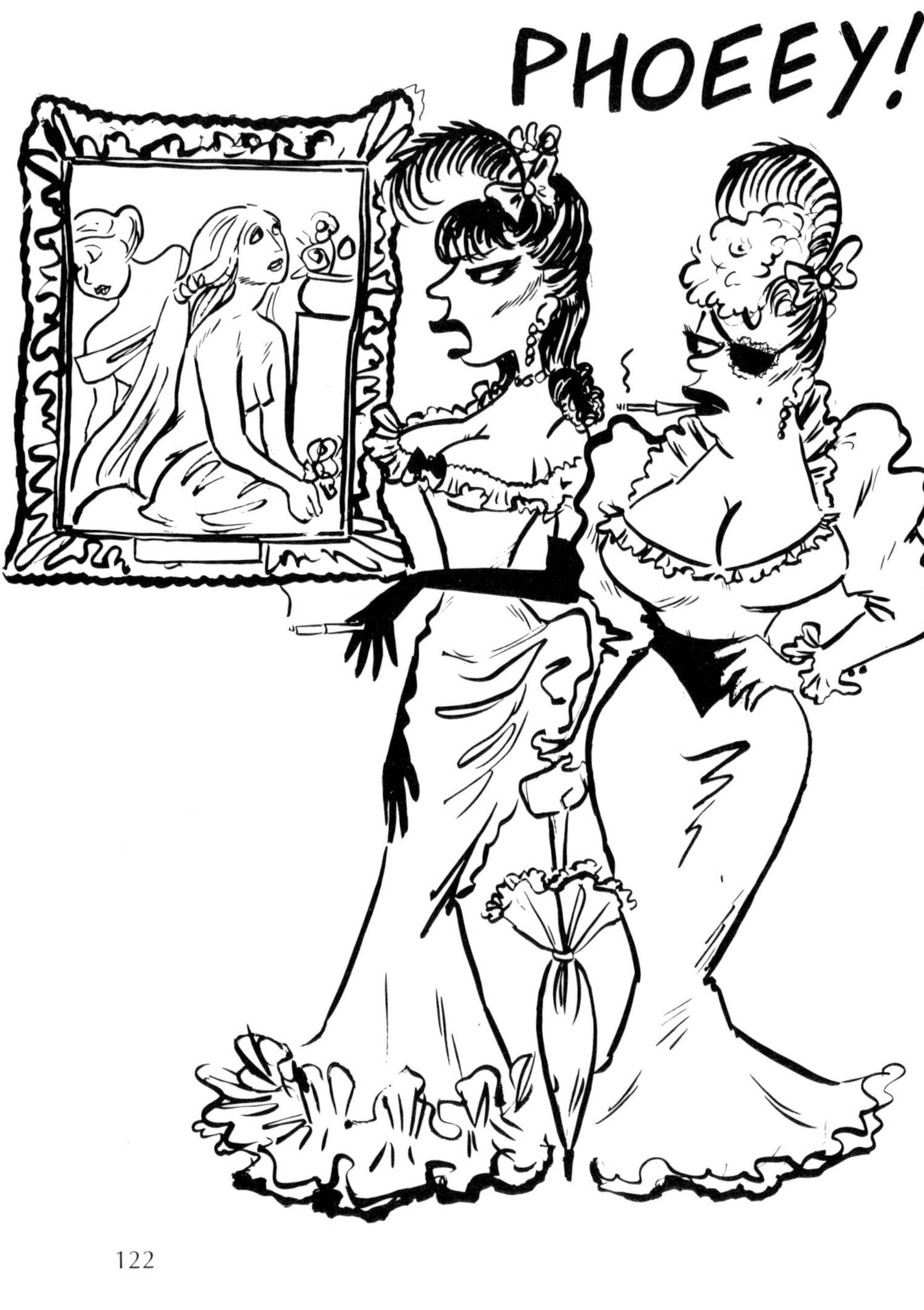
PHOEEY!

The passive pose of Cabanel's *Venus* is in complete contrast to the elevated position and raised head of *Olympia*. Manet has fashioned her to display self-possession, and she stares out at the (male) spectator, meeting his gaze and creating a self-consciousness in the voyeuristic viewer that Cabanel wants to avoid.

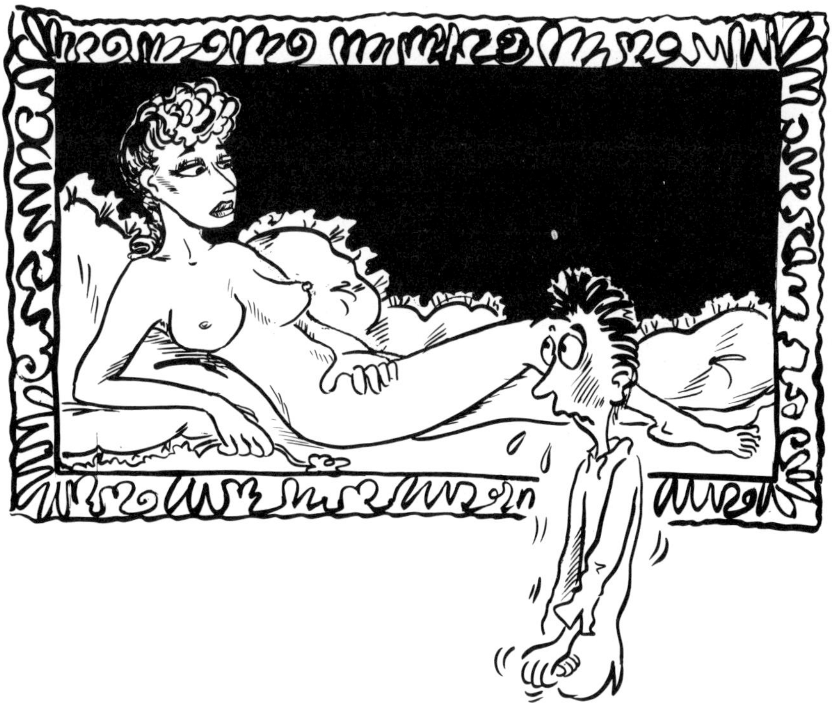

'The Nude' is a distinct and long established theme in Western art — indeed Manet anchors *Olympia* to tradition by making several conscious references in the picture to Titian's *Venus of Urbino* (1538). Instead of breaking with tradition outright, Manet acknowledges tradition even as he undermines it; he lays bare its conventions by a selective departure from them.

Manet's work is not more 'realistic' than Cabanel's — social reality is still mediated in *Olympia* by the language of art. But Manet aids the spectator's understanding of the real world by revealing how other *art* has misrepresented the reality of women's lives. At the time Manet was painting, modesty and virginity were regarded as prime female virtues, yet prostitution was rife and the walls of the Salon were covered with images of female flesh. *Olympia* served to unmask this hypocrisy.

Evidence that Manet had touched a raw social nerve can be found in the hostile critical reception his painting was given. The *Birth of Venus,* however, which is clearly much more erotic, was highly regarded and bought by the Emperor for his personal collection.

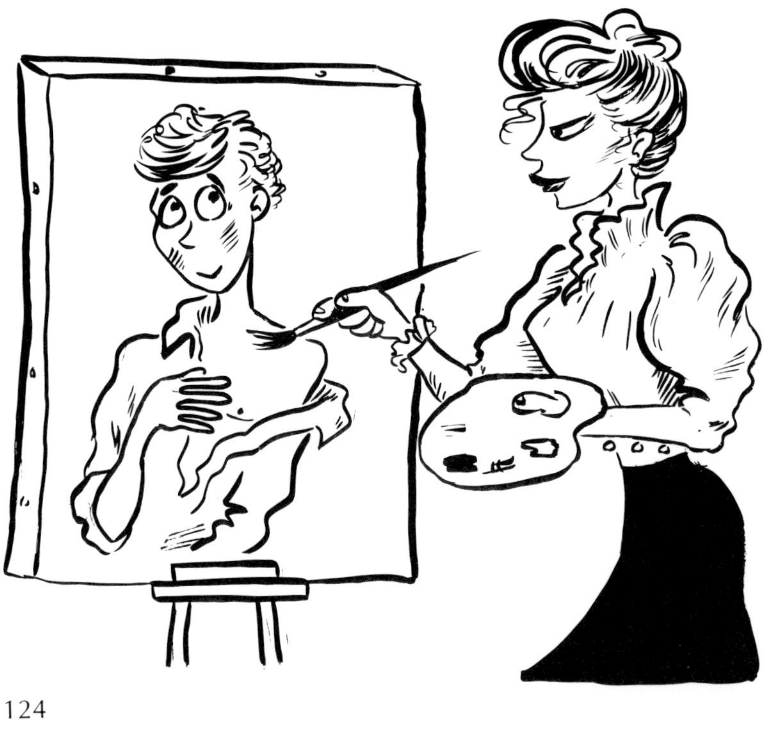

A key technique the Surrealists employed to liberate the unconscious was 'automatism'. By this they meant any procedure which helped them to by-pass conscious preconceptions and imposed habits, and hence to move beyond the known.

Originally inspired by Freud's couch method of free association, when translated into visual terms 'automatism' meant the validation of scribbling, doodling and other random means of beginning an image.

One particular type of automatism favoured by Ernst became known as 'frottage' (from the French verb *frotter*, 'to rub'). The textured surface of objects placed beneath a sheet of paper were rubbed through. These suggested to the imagination entirely new images, which were then clarified by further working. Some evidence of the original source material was usually retained, however, bringing a richness of association to the final result.

The basics of this technique will be familiar from childhood art-play, and this is something that would have delighted the Surrealists. They believed that creativity is the province of all, and anything which punctured the mystique of the artist, the aura of high art, was welcomed by them as undermining authority.

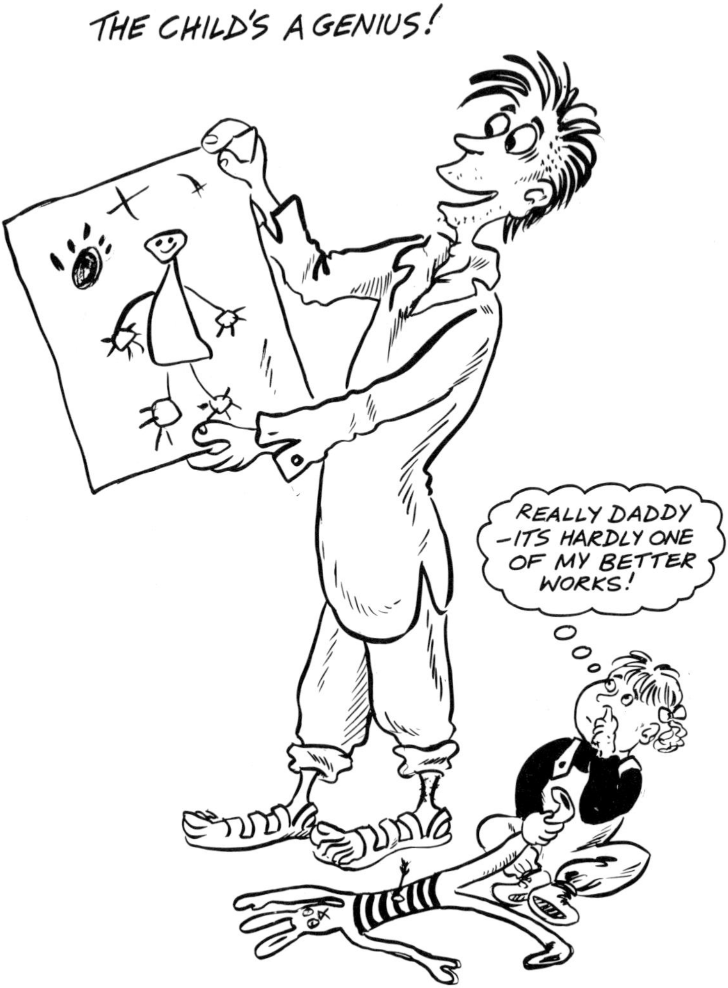

Although the Surrealists adopted automatism with a socially critical goal in mind, later artists, including the US painter Jackson Pollock, were to find it a valuable means of stimulating creativity even when more narrowly artistic goals were being pursued.

It was for paintings such as *Yellow Islands* that Pollock became famous, and labelled as 'Jack the Dripper'.

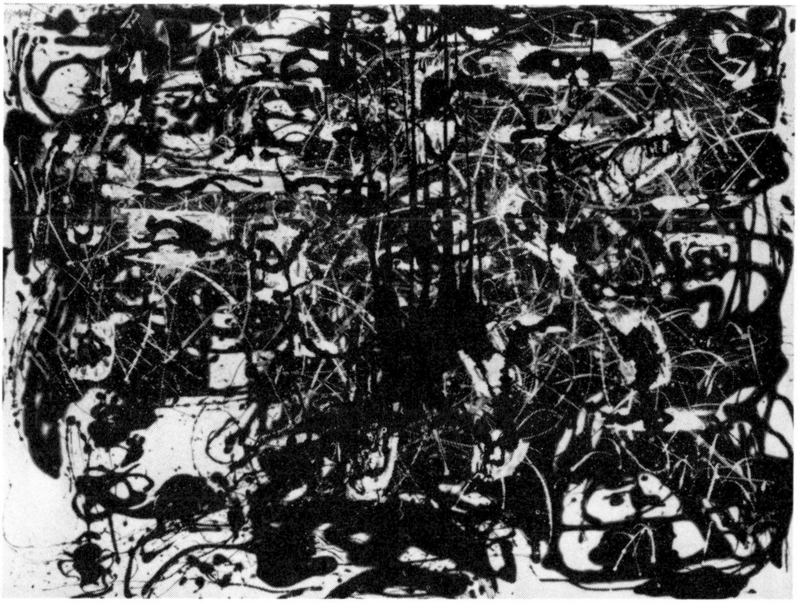
Jackson Pollock *Yellow Islands* 1952

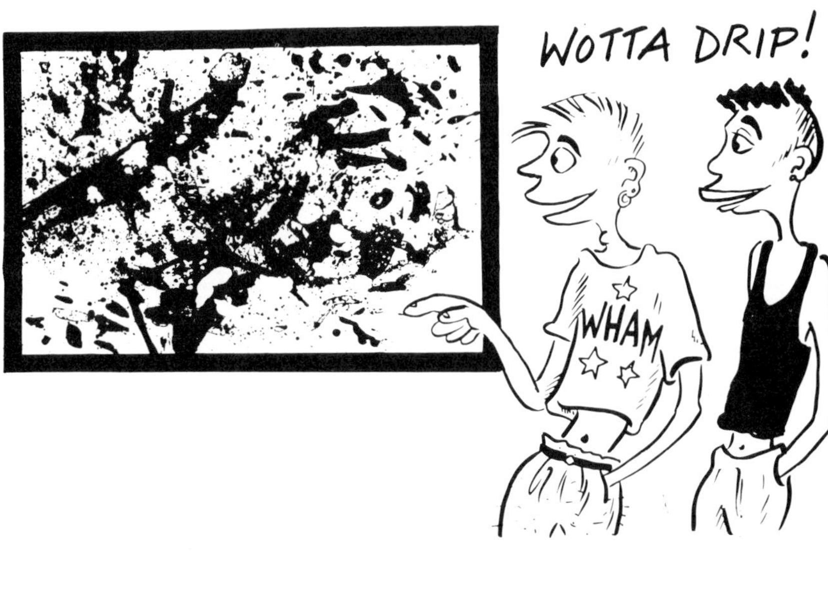

As that pejorative label indicates, Pollock's technique and the questions about artistic skill that it raises have been the major barrier to a wider appreciation of his work. In particular, considerable confusion (and hilarity) has been generated by the somewhat unorthodox techniques he adopted — for example, the fact that he typically laid his canvas out on the floor, rather than standing it up on an easel, and dripped paint from pots instead of applying it with a brush. It was even claimed that he rode a bicycle around on his pictures (he didn't). It is often alleged that such idiosyncratic methods involved no skill or control, and that his ambition was simply to let chance alone decide what happened in the image. So, what's the truth?

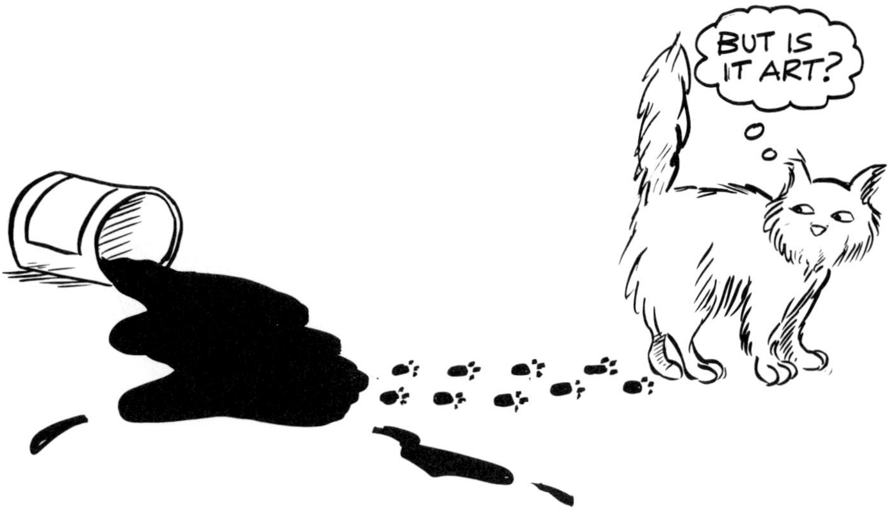

Although it may be more comfortable to believe in objective standards of skill in art (which would give us an easy way out of the difficult task of assessing quality), we can only talk about skill in relation to a specific end. When Pollock pours his paint onto a canvas which has been laid out on the studio floor he is simply using the most suitable means to achieve his particular goal.

Pollock's chosen method enables the creation of a fluid, continuous line. (A brush, which requires periodic reloading with paint, can only provide an intermittent line.) And pouring also allows a *faster* approach to working — an interest in a rapidity of mark-making probably stemmed from Pollock's encounter with the Surrealists' use of automatism to outpace the censorship of the rational conscious mind.

On the large scale that Pollock preferred to work (*Yellow Islands* is 144cm by 185cm) small, fastidious gestures would have been lost, so pouring enabled him to create marks of the appropriate size and energy, using motions of the whole arm and not merely of the hand.

Working with the canvas flat on the floor is perfectly comprehensible as a logical consequence of a decision to pour the paint. On a vertical surface his marks would immediately drip and hence destroy themselves, and gravity would hinder rather than help the application of paint. The 'weightless' feel Pollock's paintings acquire when hung vertically is partially due to the freedom his working method also gave him to approach the canvas from all sides.

What of the charge that Pollock's paintings are nothing but the result of accident? Chance effects are undoubtedly present in Pollock's painting, but these have been consciously provoked and consciously accepted, and thus in an important sense they have been actively *willed.* In any case, absolute control is never present in art. Even the finest brush is not entirely subject to our direction in the marks that it makes. It's the same in life: our carefully-laid and logical plans do not always come to fruition; forces intervene that are beyond our control and our ability to predict.

Instead of inflexibly resisting the inevitable intrusion of random factors, Pollock was willing to meet the accidental head on. He invited it into his art as a positive opportunity for creating surprise, confident that ultimately it could be tamed for an artistic purpose. His open-ended approach to the creative process was conceived as a dialogue — in his words, an 'easy give and take' — with his materials. He was happy to begin painting with only a 'general notion' of what he was about, since in this frame of mind there was more chance of an encounter with the unknown.

Despite the apparent novelty and 'difficulty' of Pollock's methods, looked at from another point of view they are very accessible. Although pouring paint is not the commonest method of creating an image, we can hardly say that Pollock is using a technique which is outside our normal experience — as any child who has dripped treacle onto porridge can tell you. In short, there is a lucidity to Pollock's art in the sense that we can see and clearly understand how the paintings are made — contrast this with many old master techniques that are a mystery to all but the initiated.

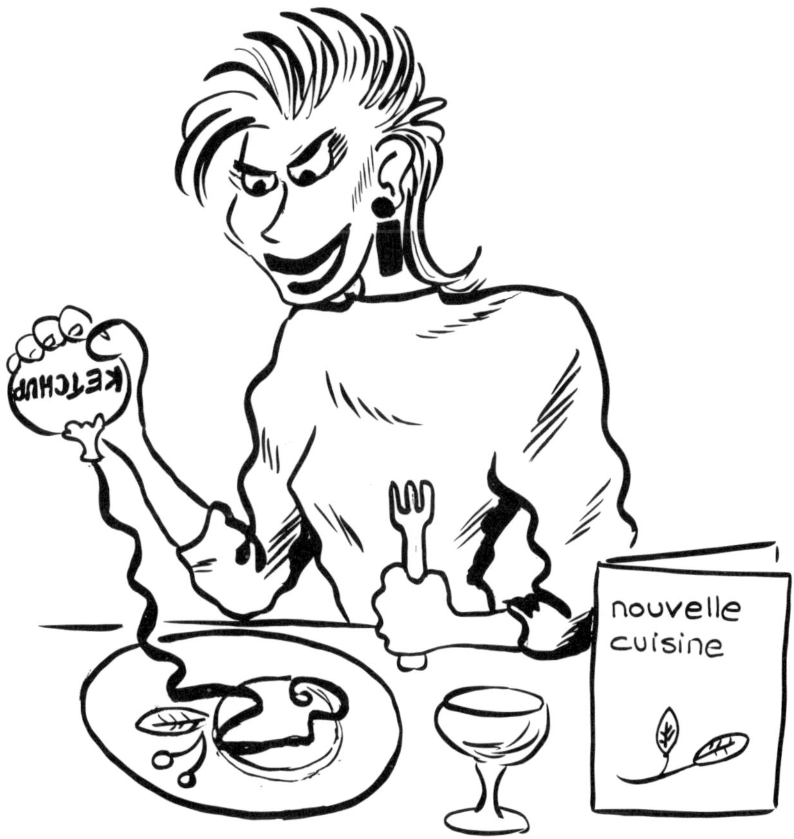

Moveover, his work is in many respects perfectly continuous with traditional practices in art. Most obviously, Pollock has chosen to stick with the same materials that artists have favoured for centuries: paint and canvas. This conservative dimension to his art helps preserve the conditions in which communication can take place; we are familiar with the properties of these materials and the type of expressive effects they have been made to carry in the past. (Incidentally, there *is* a degree of dexterity involved in his method of pouring the paint.)

What matters finally is how the paintings themselves hold up, not how the artist got the paint onto the canvas. After all, Titian frequently used his fingers instead of brushes in his late works. And if you think about it, using hairs from an animal attached to a piece of a tree can seem a pretty strange way of applying your paint.

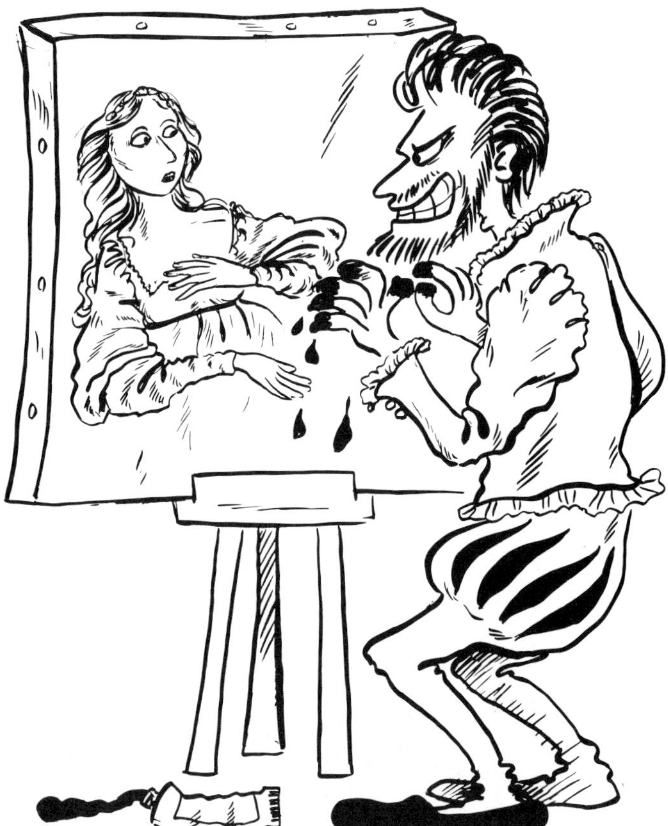

I would argue that the best of Pollock's work has a formal order and visual complexity which makes it perfectly reasonable for us to discuss it in a similar manner to the images of artists such as Picasso or Mondrian.

Of course, there are some differences between them.

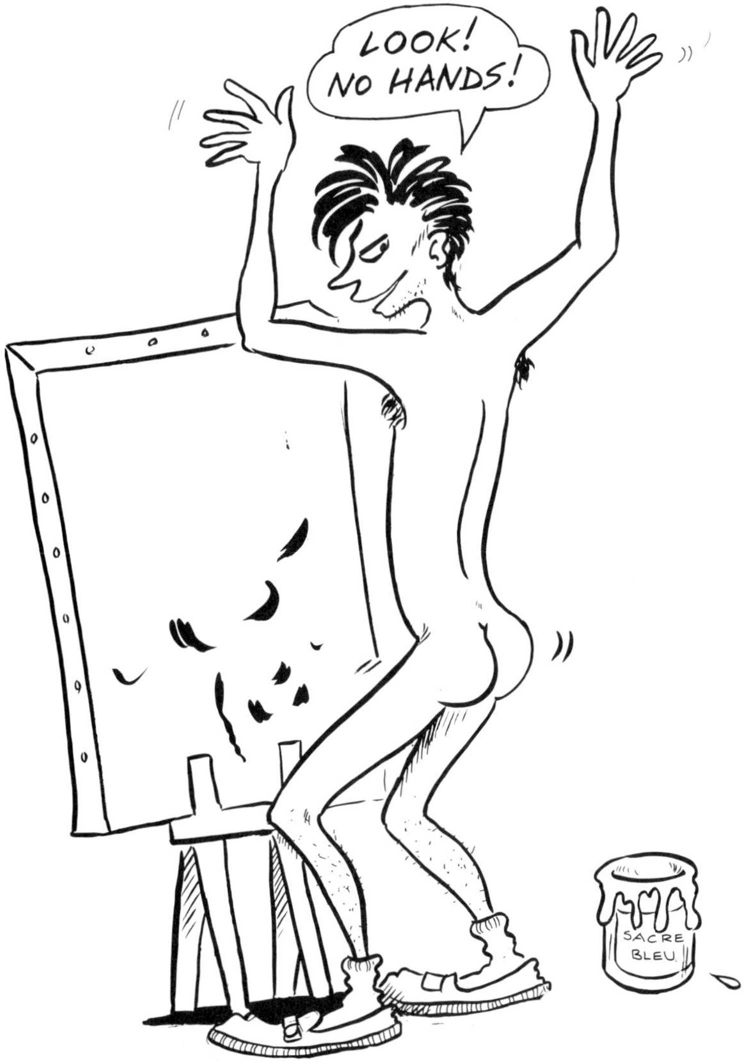

For example, the 'rules' of compositional harmony tend to vary from one artist to another. Whereas architectural metaphors might be appropriate to characterize Picasso's or Mondrian's notions of pictorial order, *ecological* analogies might work better with Pollock. Although Picasso's and Mondrian's images have the look of being constructed additively out of distinct formal fragments, we read Pollock's picture at a single glance as a rhythmic unity. There is usually no hierarchy of importance among the forms in the painting. Instead, a homogeneity is created by the repetition of similar linear gestures all over the surface.

On the other hand, there are important similarities. For instance, the uniformity of treatment usually present in Pollock's paintings helps establish an awareness of the flat plane of the canvas surface, something that Picasso and Mondrian also valued. And again like these other two artists, Pollock wants to give us a sense of three-dimensional space as well, albeit one that is achieved without illusionistic means. In his poured works he makes it difficult for us to disentangle the varous skeins of paint entirely (so we are prevented from securing a coherent reading of space which would abolish our consciousness of the picture plane), but by giving them different colours Pollock creates hints of *overlap*, and hence of an undefined space.

The effect is often enhanced by the distribution of the paint. A greater density of paint towards the centre of the image can make it seem to bulge forward — suggesting a virtual space as much in front of the canvas as behind it. Although at the borders of the painting (where the bare canvas shows through) most gestures acknowledge the framing edge, leading our eye back into the image and helping to create its formal unity, some escape and provide hints of a greater space beyond the frame.

Our case studies of the work of the Surrealists and of Manet have enabled us to discuss artists who attempted to create a socially critical art using modern styles. That our investigation of Pollock's painting has caused us to stray from the issue of politics and modern art only parallels the way modern artists themselves have tended to surrender such concerns. Let us return to a consideration of political issues and ask whether 'modern' or 'realistic' styles are most useful to a politicized art.

Although artistic radicalism and social radicalism are often confused, clearly modernistic art is not *innately* politically progressive.

The Italian Futurists may have been responsible for certain innovations concerning the representation of movement in the static world of art, but they supported a militaristic outlook and their art ultimately became aligned with Mussolini's Fascism.

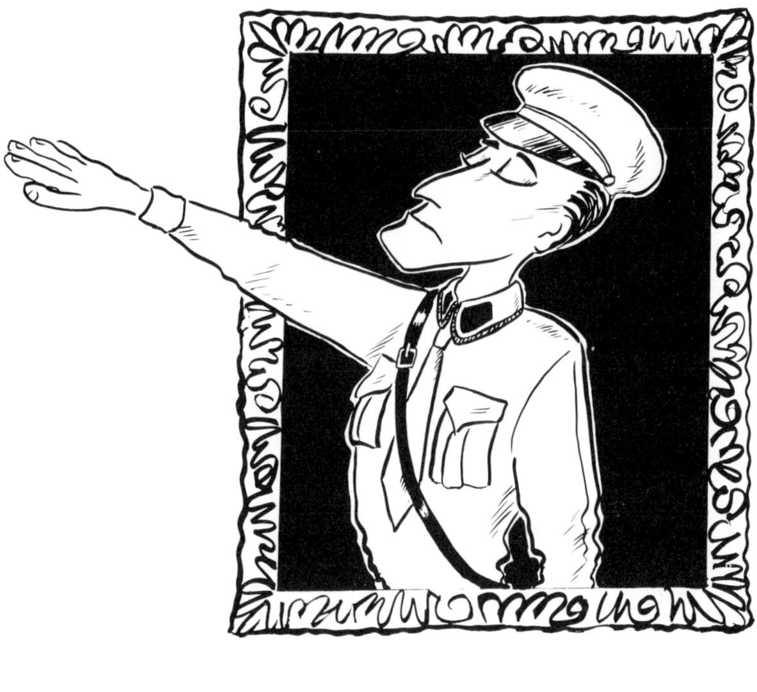

Picasso's *Guernica* of 1937 shows the artist attempting to make an overtly political painting. The impetus was an episode in the Spanish Civil War where planes supplied to Franco's Nationalist Army by Germany bombed the Republican Basque town of that name, with devastating results.

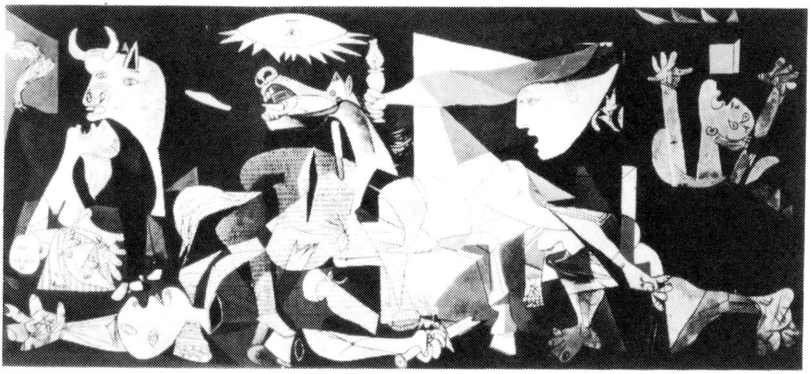

Pablo Picasso *Guernica* 1937

Although the work may be seen as an effective generalized statement about the horrors of war, how well does it function as a committed political act?

Political intentions are not found in Picasso's earlier art, and the Cubistic language he uses here was not developed with such a purpose in mind. Indeed, it seems strained when applied to this new objective. Surely if art is to serve a propaganda goal it must present a clear message? Yet here there is no reference to modern warfare let alone to the atrocity that had been comitted by the Fascists.

Perhaps most styles of modern art are innately unsuited to a propaganda function — they certainly tend to be unsuitable in practice since they are not widely understood at present. If we define the notion of 'political art' in a narrow and crudely utilitarian way it is indeed difficult to see a significant role for modernistic languages of art.

Yet things are different if we broaden our idea of oppositional art to include anything which can make us critically aware of the social world in which we live, as discussion of the Surrealists and of Manet should have shown. For art to exercise a political function in this larger sense it is not even necessary for the artist to have a programmatic political goal in mind; a certain clear-sightedness about the world and a desire to share that insight through art might be enough.

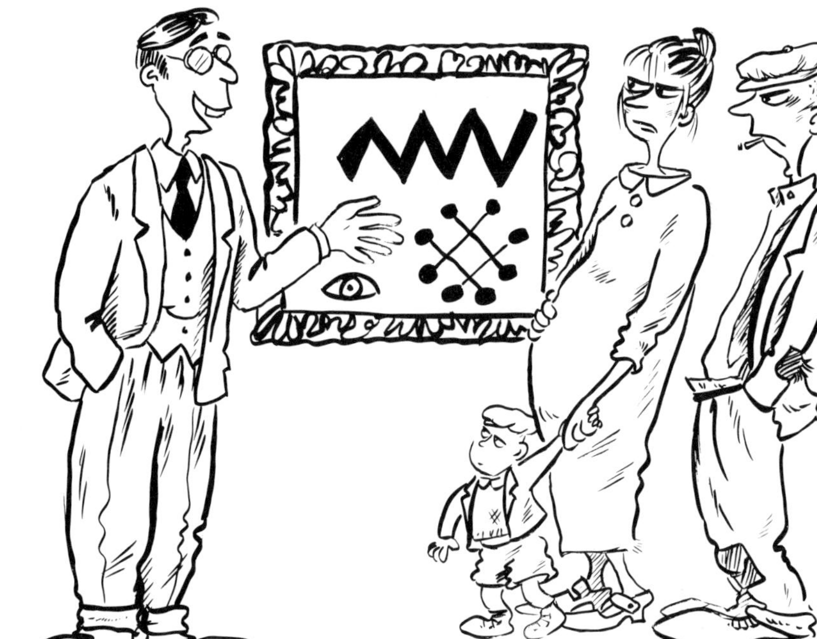

What modern art lacks in accessibility it can make up for in sophistication and adaptability. It provides an elaborated code capable of making subtle distinctions and precise comments, and this is as valuable when it is used for political tasks as in any other role. It permits parody and irony, for instance.

Unlike much 'realistic' art, modernism adopts a critical and self-aware relationship to 'the traditional' in art. Modern art has built into it an awareness that art is conventional, that it cannot be taken as providing an objectively 'true' image of life but an interested, blinkered one. Although we can learn to think about all imagery in this way, 'realistic' art can more easily be used to deceive us that we are seeing a 'transparent' reflection of the world, and not merely someone's claim about it. 'Realistic' art doesn't invite us to question its language, to disclose the assumptions buried within it.

This limitation of 'realistic' styles is perhaps most evident with photography, which is commonly regarded as a reliable source of information about the world. We are often told that 'the camera cannot lie', but even here choices concerning form have to be made (as we saw at the beginning of this book).

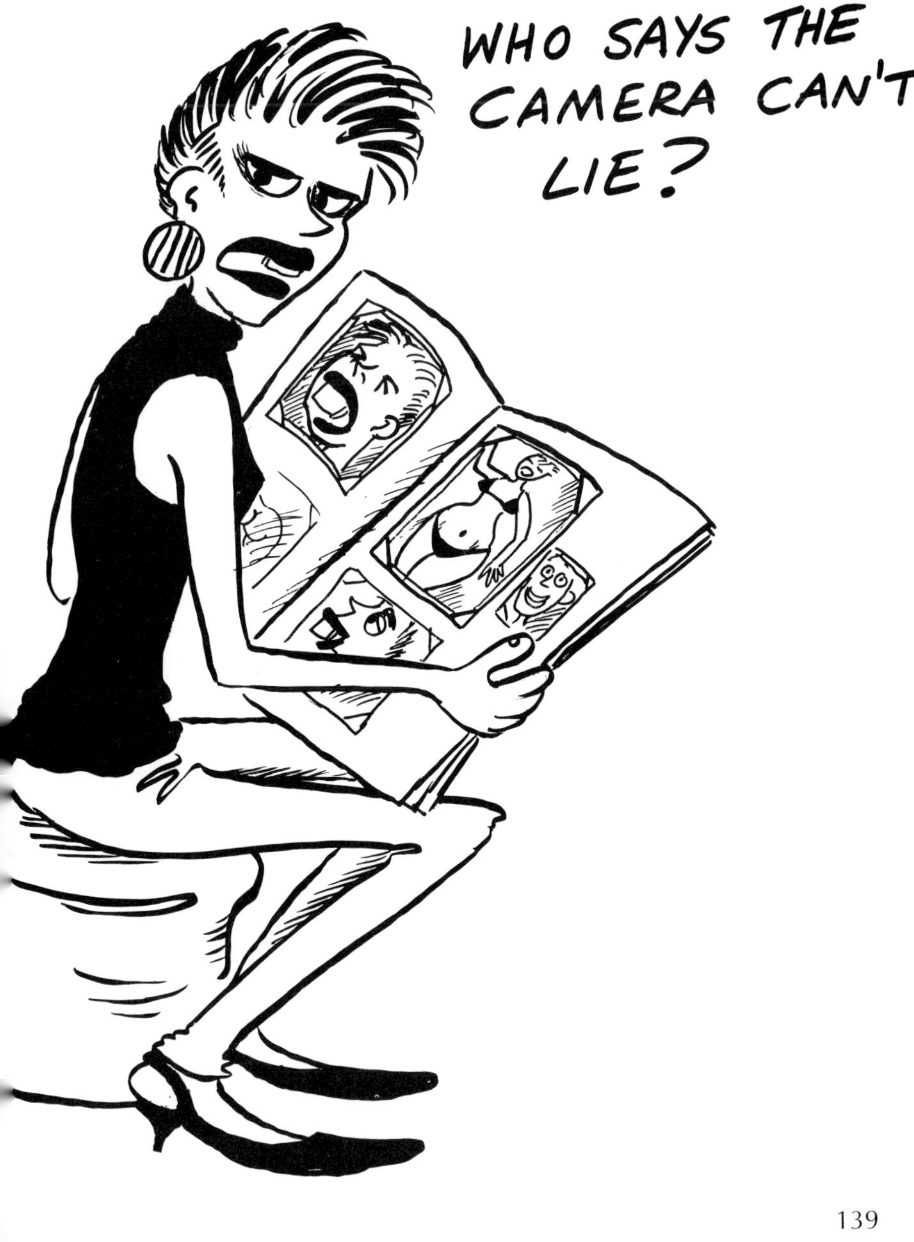
WHO SAYS THE CAMERA CAN'T LIE?

Formal decisions — the issue of 'how' rather than 'what' — can (consciously or unconsciously) affect the political impact of an image — and make the difference, for instance, between a reclining female nude by Cabanel and one by Manet. A photo or a 'realistic' painting showing an ostensibly political subject such as poverty could prompt us to question the social causes of poverty (and even suggest what these causes might be), but it could also represent poverty as merely a sad but inevitable fact of life, even a picturesque pretext for us to wallow self-indulgently in pity.

I do not mean to imply that photography or 'realistic' styles of painting lack a critical potential. In the hands of Gustave Courbet, for example, realistic painting certainly did have one. Although, remember that in the mid-19th century his 'realism' *was* avant-garde or modernistic — it presented a challenging new way of seeing the world. The

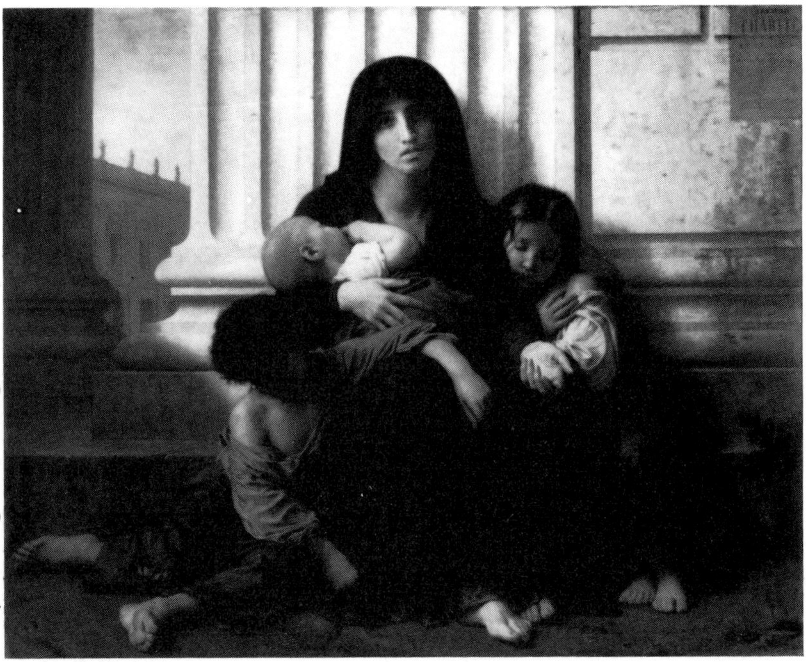

Adolphe Bouguereau *Indigent Family* 1885

point is that 'realism' isn't *necessarily* critical, and in our own century has frequently been anything but.

In Stalin's Russia the preoccupation of modern artists with form was deemed an irrelevant distraction from a concern with social content. In Nazi Germany modern art was labelled as 'decadent'. Both these authoritarian regimes consciously privileged 'realistic' styles. In Russia, 'Socialist Realism' became a tool for *mis*representing the actual conditions of life. Rather than drawing attention to contradictions and imperfections in society, it marketed under the banner of 'realism' larger than life idealizations of Soviet life that served the interests of those in power.

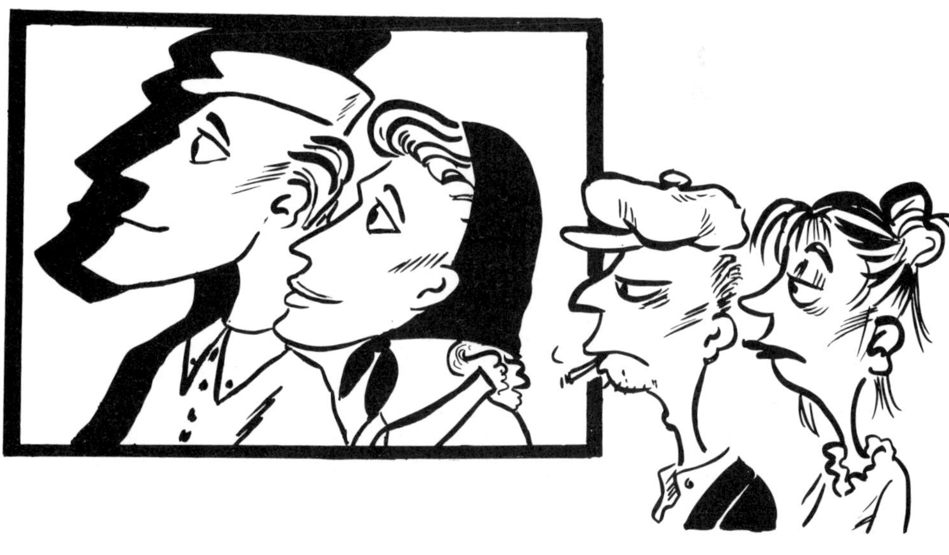

Socialist Realism, like its Nazi equivalent and indeed like much so-called 'realistic' art of this century, tends to deal in visual clichés. Instead of an art which has been born of a discriminating encounter with the world, we are offered a frozen art which relies on received notions. The restricted codes of popular art often employ in a bastardized, unexamined way conventions borrowed from 'high' art (conventions which in their own time may have been contentious and of appeal to a minority only)).

Modernistic painting and sculpture which attempts to be socially critical runs the risk of failing to communicate — of outrunning its audience by leaving behind the commonly-used languages of art. But an art which follows — indeed, panders to — existing taste, is liable to be conservative because of the limitations it must submit to. The price of accessibility can be triviality.

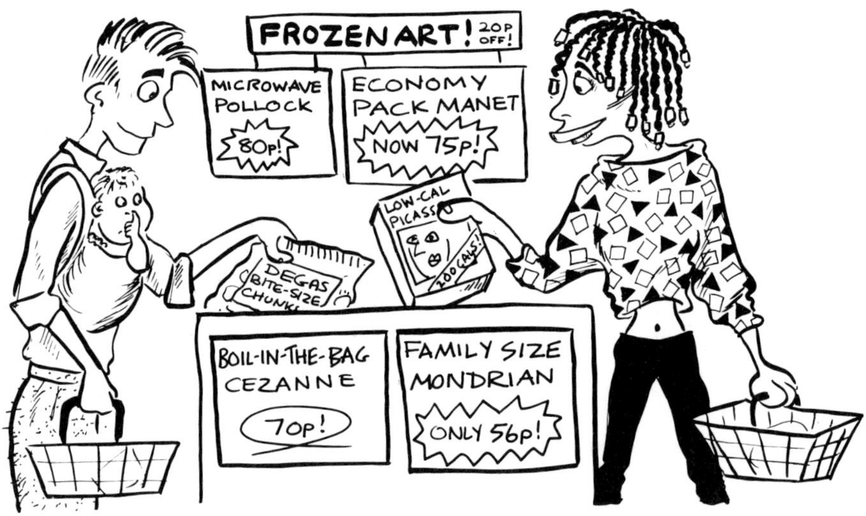

'Popular' art is usually popular only in the sense that it is produced *for* the many. It is still the art *of* the powerful few since it serves their interests. Such art is typically:

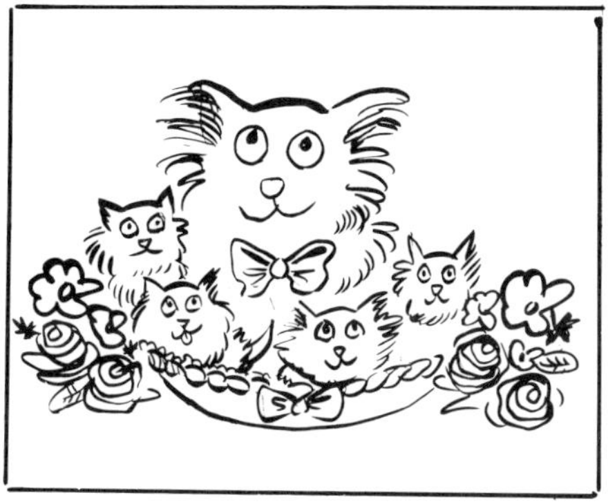

sentimental . . .

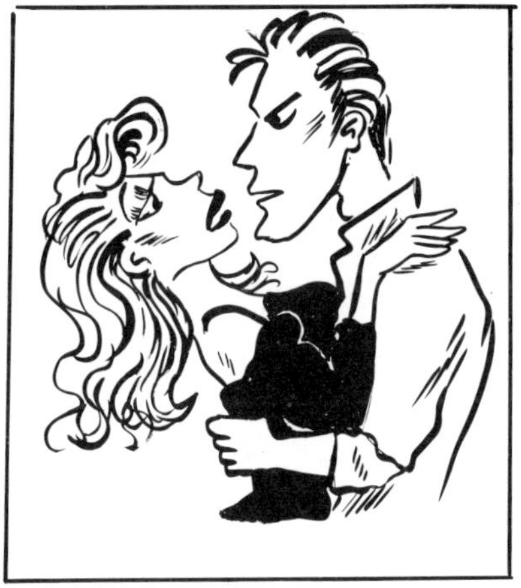

idealised . . .

pornographic . . .

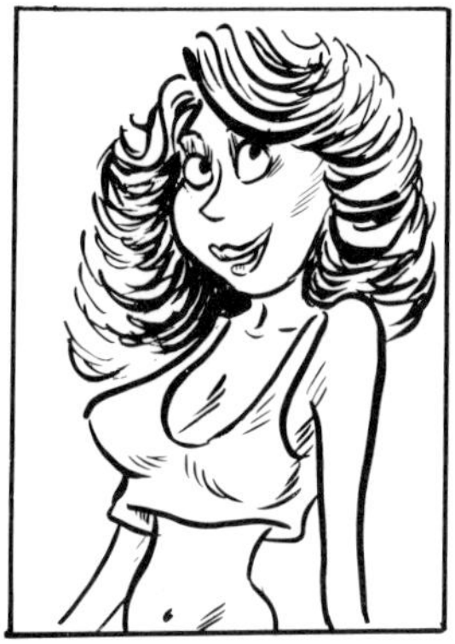

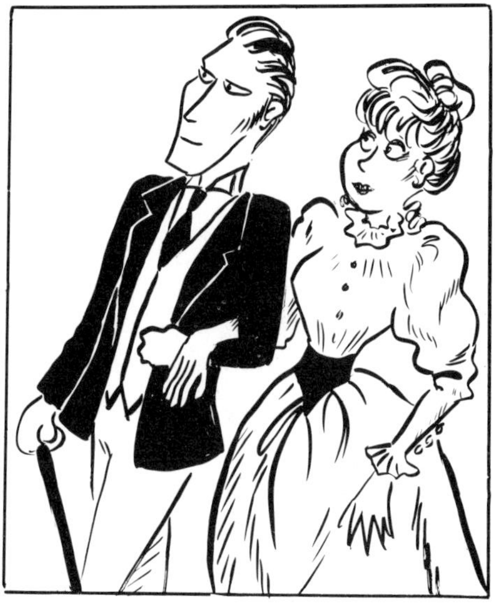

or nostalgic . . .

Ultimately, neither 'modern' nor 'realistic' styles can be regarded as inherently more suitable than the other for the task of creating a socially critical art. To assert that 'realistic' ways of painting should always prevail is (paradoxically) to be overconcerned with an issue of form — the very accusation that is so commonly made against 'modern' artists. Instead, we should give priority to *function* and ask which style is better suited to the particular task in hand. A pluralistic approach is needed. A multiplicity of styles is in itself an advantage, providing greater resources on which to draw.

The economic and social dynamic of history will inevitably produce changes in the context in which art operates. The adoption of a new style can be a response to altered historical circumstances, and in the field of political art (as in any other) the effectiveness of an idiom can change over time. For instance, the voicing of personal feelings of alienation such as we find in expressionistic art could function as a political act at one point in time, yet be an episode of reactionary subjectivism at another.

One particular factor in this shifting historical context is the response of vested interests in society to attempts at criticism of the status quo. Modern capitalist society has moved to counteract and neutralize critical initiatives in the cultural sphere and this ability to adapt is one reason why a political art needs more than one string to its bow; it needs a continuing resourcefulness about means and a willingness to innovate.

Censorship is only one strategy for outlawing art which might upset the status quo. Denial of patronage provides an equally efficient barrier. Any art which survives this discouragement can be dismissed as degenerate or childish, thus deterring people from making the effort to uncover the messages it might contain. A more sophisticated tactic is practised in democratic societies which pride themselves on their liberalism, where politically radical art (such as that of the Surrealists) can quite successfully be invalidated by its elevation into a depoliticized category of 'Art'.

The sanitization of political art is carried out on a physical level by the confinement of art objects to the luxurious ghetto of the art gallery or museum.

This actual separation of art from the rest of social life is supported intellectually by the dominant theories of modern art criticism. Such criticism tends to claim for art an *absolute* (rather than a relative) autonomy, giving priority to formal issues over those of content. Some artists, such as Frank Stella, *are* solely concerned with form, but it's not true of them all. Such theories — which have been labelled 'Modernistic' — overlook the desire of those such as the Surrealists, Cubists and Manet to refer in their work to the world outside of art, and play down the role of extra-artistic forces (including art criticism itself) in shaping art.

Successfully neutralized and incorporated, a modern art becomes of positive use to a society's ruling elite, a badge declaring its cultured liberalism.

When the Museum of Modern Art in New York staged international travelling shows of work by Pollock and other US artists in the 1950s such art became a Cold War weapon, a symbol of the 'freedom' and individualism of capitalist society and a comment on cultural repression in the Communist bloc.

An important role in the founding and running of the Museum of Modern Art has been played by the Rockefeller family, and they provide a particularly concrete example of the ways in which the economic, political and cultural worlds can become linked. The family fortune was accumulated by John D. Rockefeller Snr through a US oil industry monopoly. His daughter-in-law, Abby Aldrich Rockefeller, was a co-founder of MOMA and a trustee till the end of her life. Her son, Nelson Rockefeller, was a US vice-president and a governor of New York, as well as being a trustee and one-time president of MOMA.

In the history of modern art which MOMA's diplays embody, US art has much larger wall space than that devoted to the painting and sculpture of post-revolutionary Russia.

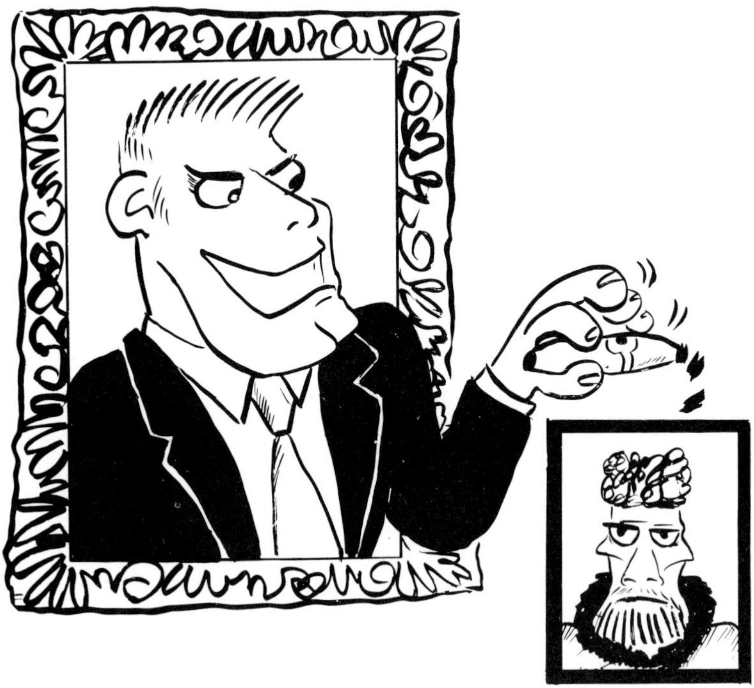

That the art of any age tends to embody the interests of the power and uphold existing social relations is reason enough why this area of human activity should receive our close attention. But I hope also to have demonstrated that modern art contains an accumulated experience of the world that repays the effort involved in becoming 'literate' in its codes. How we represent our world (or how others represent it for us) is intimately linked with how we are able to see that world, and hence with how we are to act in it.

GOING FURTHER

I have avoided a 'Great Artists' or 'Movements in Modern Art' approach in this book, preferring instead to tackle specific themes and issues. Chronological accounts can be found in 22 and 27; 32 breaks the period down by movement; 13 is a useful anthology of artists' statements. Consult the bibliographies of these books for more detailed studies of particular artists and movements.

Neither have I discussed very recent art. This was partly due to a shortage of space and partly because I believe that artists are still working within the basic parameters of the modern movement. (Most authors in 16 would disagree.) Writing about recent art tends to be more critical than historical, and has a tendency to date quickly. 5,6 and 7 are useful anthologies of critical texts, but are heavily biased towards the USA. 29 brings together writing about Pop art.

Of those texts which question the dominant interpretation of modern art, 29 has the widest chronological sweep (from Manet to Pollock), 14, 15 (the latter dealing with Manet and Impressionism) give the most detailed case studies. Anthologies (1, 5, 6, 7, 9, 10, 12, 13, 16, 18, 19, 23, 26, 19, 31, 32, 33, 34) are an economical way of gaining a multiplicity of perspectives on a topic. Periodicals can also fulfil this role; in particular, *Screen* (British Film Institute) and *Block* (Middlesex Polytechnic) have included important debates about aspects of visual culture.

For a discussion of the conventionality of representation which draws on lessons of psychology, 20 is a basic text. A differing, philosophically-based view is given in 21; 36 is written by a philosopher, 17 argues that the unquestioned belief in our ability to transparently represent the world was the characteristic of a particular historical era, when it was shared by all fields of knowledge. The Structuralist tradition emphasizes the codified nature of all our communication: 10 and 33 are good introductions, 4 is very readable.

Further discussion of the issue of expression is found in 19 and 21.

The dominant 'Modernist' tradition in art criticism is most clearly exemplified in the writings of Clement Greenberg. Key essays of his can be found in 18 and 19, 18 includes a critical response.

Important leftist debates concerning the arts are presented in 1; texts by Brecht and Benjamin are also included in 19. Since they mostly centre on literature rather than the visual arts, art historians must try to reapply work done in the tradition of literary criticism. 8 captures many of the issues which have risen here. 35 attempts to outline a general sociology of culture compatible with a historical materialist position, but with the major examples taken from literature.

A theory of culture which sees it neither as having an absolute autonomy from politics, nor as being a mere 'reflection' of the economic base of society, has much to learn from the ideas of Antonio Gramsci. 10 combines extracts from his writings with a useful discussion of their applicability. 2 develops a similar analysis to his, and explicitly attempts to apply it to the arts. 8 is critical.

Further information about the politics of US art and art institutions can be found in 18.

In recent years, feminist views and theories have challenged traditional attitudes to art and its history. 11 is an introduction to the analysis of women's place in art today and yesterday; 30 goes into more detail. 26 catalogues the shocks women's art has caused the contemporary art system.

If we see the term 'Art' as referring to a specific, historically relative category rather than to some transhistorical 'essence' then we may wish to look at other forms of visual culture in our society (and consider how theoretical tools used to evaluate them might be applied in traditional art history). 25 provides a basic guide to the way in which film mediates reality; 3 raises issues of film theory, including the question of realism, as does 9 (which also considers T.V.). 24 considers the visual style of youth cultures, which are also mentioned in 10. The relationship between 'high' and 'popular' culture is discussed by Greenberg and Crow in 18, and also preoccupies Adorno (1).

12 discusses new developments in art history.

1. *Aesthetics and Politics, Debates between Bloch, Lukacs, Brecht, Benjamin, Adorno,* Verso, 1980.
2. L. Althusser, *Essays on Ideology,* Verso, 1984.
3. J. D. Andrew, *The Major Film Theories,* Oxford University Press, 1978.
4. R. Barthes, *Mythologies,* Jonathan Cape, 1972.
5. G. Battcock (ed.), *Idea Art. A Critical Anthology,*Dutton, 1968.
6. G. Battcock (ed.), *Minimal Art. A Critical Anthology,* Dutton 1968.
7. G. Battcock (ed.), *The New Art. A Critical Anthology,* Dutton, 1973.
8. T. Bennett, *Formalism and Marxism,* Methuen, 1979.
9. T. Bennett, S. Boyd-Bowman, C. Mercer & J. Woollacott (eds), *Popular Television and Film,* British Film Institute, 1981.
10. T. Bennett, G. Martin, C. Mercer & J. Woollacott (eds), *Culture, Ideology and Social Process,* Open University Press, 1981.
11. F. Borzello & N. Ledwidge, *Women Artists. A Graphic Guide,* Camden Press, 1986.
12. F. Borzello & A. L. Rees (eds), *The New Art History,*Camden Press, 1986.
13. H. B. Chipp, *Theories of Modern Art,* University of California Press, 1968.
14. T. J. Clark, *Image of the People: Gustave Courbet and the 1848 Revolution,* Thames and Hudson, 1973.

15. T. J. Clark, *The Painting of Modern Life,* Thames and Hudson, 1985.

16. H. Foster (ed.), *Postmodern Culture,* Pluto Press, 1985.

17. M. Foucault, *The Order of Things,* Tavistock Publications, 1970.

18. F. Frascina (ed.), *Pollock and After: The Critical Debate,* Harper and Row, 1985.

19. F. Frascina & C. Harrison (eds), *Modern Art and Modernism: A Critical Anthology,* Harper and Row, 1982.

20. E. Gombrich, *Art and Illusion,* Phaidon, 1960.

21. N. Goodman, *Languages of Art,* Hackett, 1976.

22. G. H. Hamilton, *Painting and Sculpture in Europe, 1880–1940,* Penguin, 1981.

23. C. Harrison & F. Orton (eds), *Modernism, Criticism, Realism,* Harper and Row, 1984.

24. D. Hebdige, *Subculture: The Meaning of Style,* Methuen, 1979.

25. J. Izod, *Reading the Screen,* Longman/York Press, 1984.

26. S. Kent & J. Morreau (eds), *Women's Images of Men,* Writers & Readers, 1985.

27. N. Lynton, *The Story of Modern Art,* Phaidon, 1980.

28. M. Milner, *On Not Being Able to Paint,* Heinemann, 1971.

29. *Modern Art and Modernism,* Open University Press, 1983 (14 teaching packs).

30. R. Parker & G. Pollock. *Old Mistresses: Women, Art & Ideology,* Routledge, 1981.

31. J. Russell & G. Gablik (eds), *Pop Art Redefined,* Thames & Hudson, 1969.

32. N. Stangos (ed.), *Concepts of Modern Art,* Thames and Hudson, 1981.

33. J. Sturrock (ed.), *Structuralism and Since,* Oxford University Press, 1979.

34. *Towards a New Art, Essays on the Background to Abstract Art 1910–29,* The Tate Gallery, 1980.

35. R. Williams, *Culture,* Fontana, 1981.

36. R. Wollheim, *Art and its Objects,* Cambridge University Press, 1980.

WORKS REPRODUCED

59 Jackson Pollock *Yellow Islands* 1952
The Tate Gallery, London

68 Vincent Van Gogh *All Night Café* 1888
Yale University Art Gallery Bequest of Stephen Carlton Clark

71 *Whore of Babylon* woodcut from the Nuremburg Bible 15th century

80 Ernst Ludwig Kirchner *Bathers at Moritzburg* 1910-20
The Tate Gallery, London

90 George Grosz *At 5 o'clock in the Morning*
from book of drawings *The Face of the Ruling Class*
© DACS 1986

96 Paul Gauguin *Arearea (Red Dog)* 1892
Louvre, Paris

100 John Heartfield *Millions Stand Behind Me (The Meaning of the Hitler Salute)* 1932

106 George Stubbs *The Prince of Wales' Phaeton* 1793
Reproduced by Gracious Permission of her Majesty the Queen, The Queen's Collections, Windsor Castle

107 Alexander Cabanel *Birth of Venus* 1863
Louvre, Paris Photograph: Lauros-Giraudon

108 Berthe Morisot *Summer Day* 1879
Reproduced by courtesy of the Trustees The National Gallery, London

115 Salvador Dali *The Persistence of Memory* 1931
Collection, The Museum of Modern Art, New York Given anonymously © DACS 1986

119 Max Ernst plate from collage novel *A Week of Plenty* 1933 © ADAGP 1986

120 Edouard Manet *Olympia* 1865
Louvre, Paris

127 Jackson Pollock *Yellow Islands* 1952
The Tate Gallery, London

136 Pablo Picasso *Guernica* 1937
Museo del Prado, Madrid © DACS 1986

140 Adolphe Bouguereau *Indigent Family* 1985
City Museum and Art Gallery, Birmingham

ARTISTS MENTIONED IN THE TEXT

Giacomo Balla	(1871-1958)	Italy
Umberto Boccioni	(1882-1916)	Italy
Constantin Brancusi	(1876-1957)	Rumania
Adolphe Bouguereau	(1823-1889)	France
Alexandre Cabanel	(1825-1905)	France
Paul Cézanne	(1839-1906)	France
Gustave Courbet	(1819-1877)	France
Carlo Crivelli	(c. 1435-1493)	Italy
Salvador Dali	(1904-)	Spain
André Derain	(1880-1954)	France
Max Ernst	(1881-1976)	Germany
Caspar David Friedrich	(1774-1840)	Germany
Paul Gauguin	(1848-1903)	France
Vincent van Gogh	(1853-1890)	Holland
George Grosz	(1893-1959)	Germany
John Heartfield	(1891-1968)	Germany
Wassily Kandinsky	(1866-1944)	Russia
Ernst Ludwig Kirchner	(1880-1938)	Germany
René Magritte	(1898-1967)	Belgium
Edouard Manet	(1832-1883)	France
Henri Matisse	(1869-1954)	France
Joan Mirò	(1893-1983)	Spain
Piet Mondrian	(1872-1944)	Holland
Claude Monet	(1840-1926)	France
Henry Moore	(1898-1986)	England
Berthe Morisot	(1841-1895)	France
Pablo Picasso	(1881-1973)	Spain
Jackson Pollock	(1912-1956)	USA

Auguste Renoir	(1841-1919)	France
Auguste Rodin	(1840-1917)	France
Rembrandt van Ryn	(1606-1669)	Holland
George Seurat	(1859-1891)	Holland
Frank Stella	(1936-)	USA
George Stubbs	(1724-1806)	England
Titian	(c,1487-1576)	Italy
Maurice Vlaminck	(1876-1958)	France

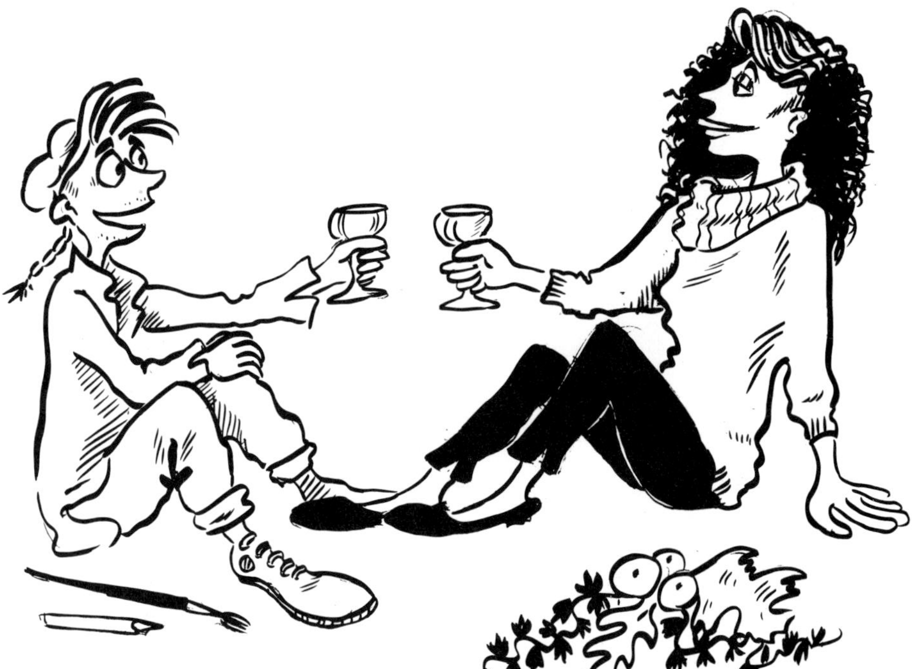

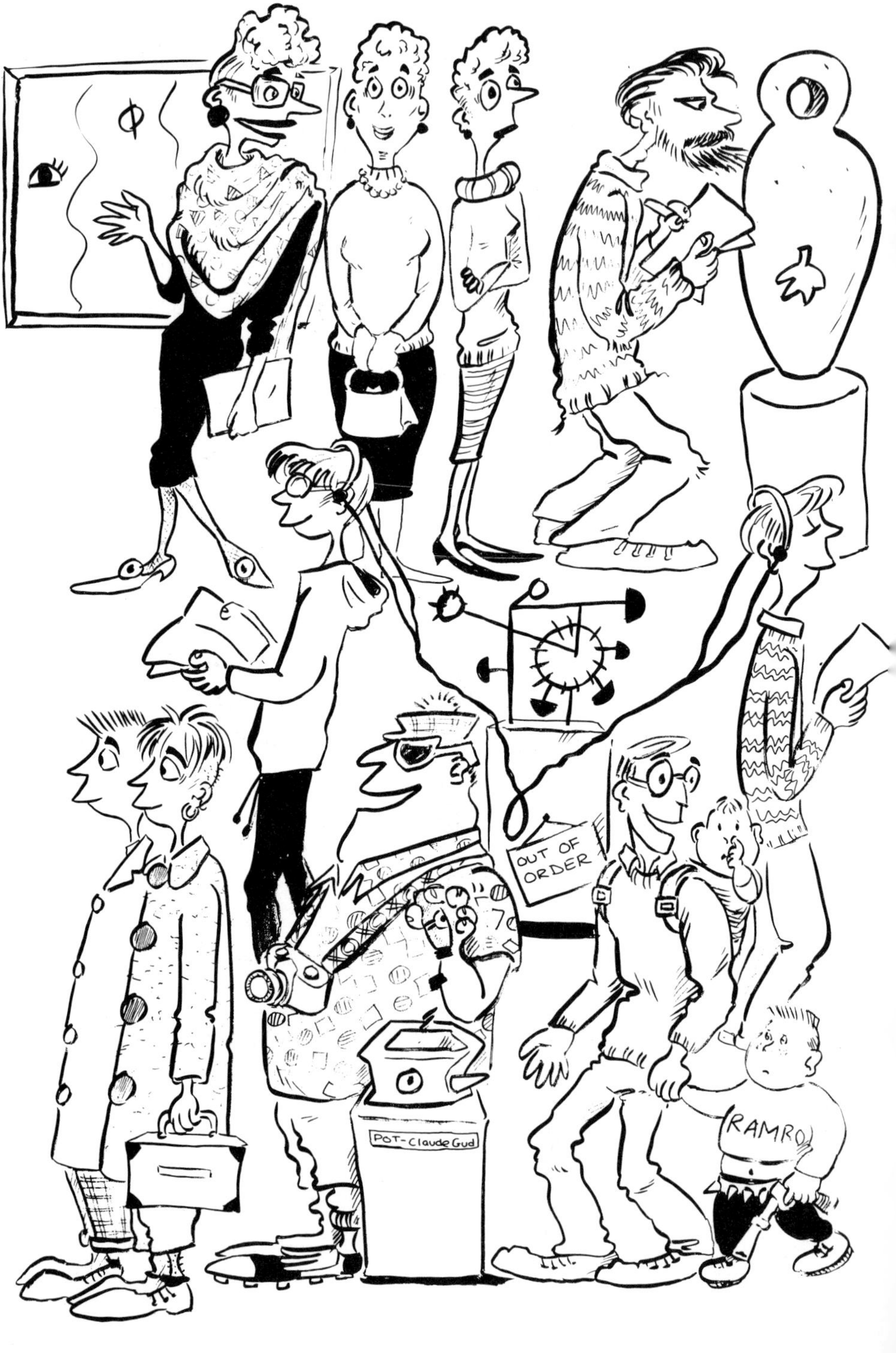
OUT OF ORDER
POT-Claude Gud
RAMRO

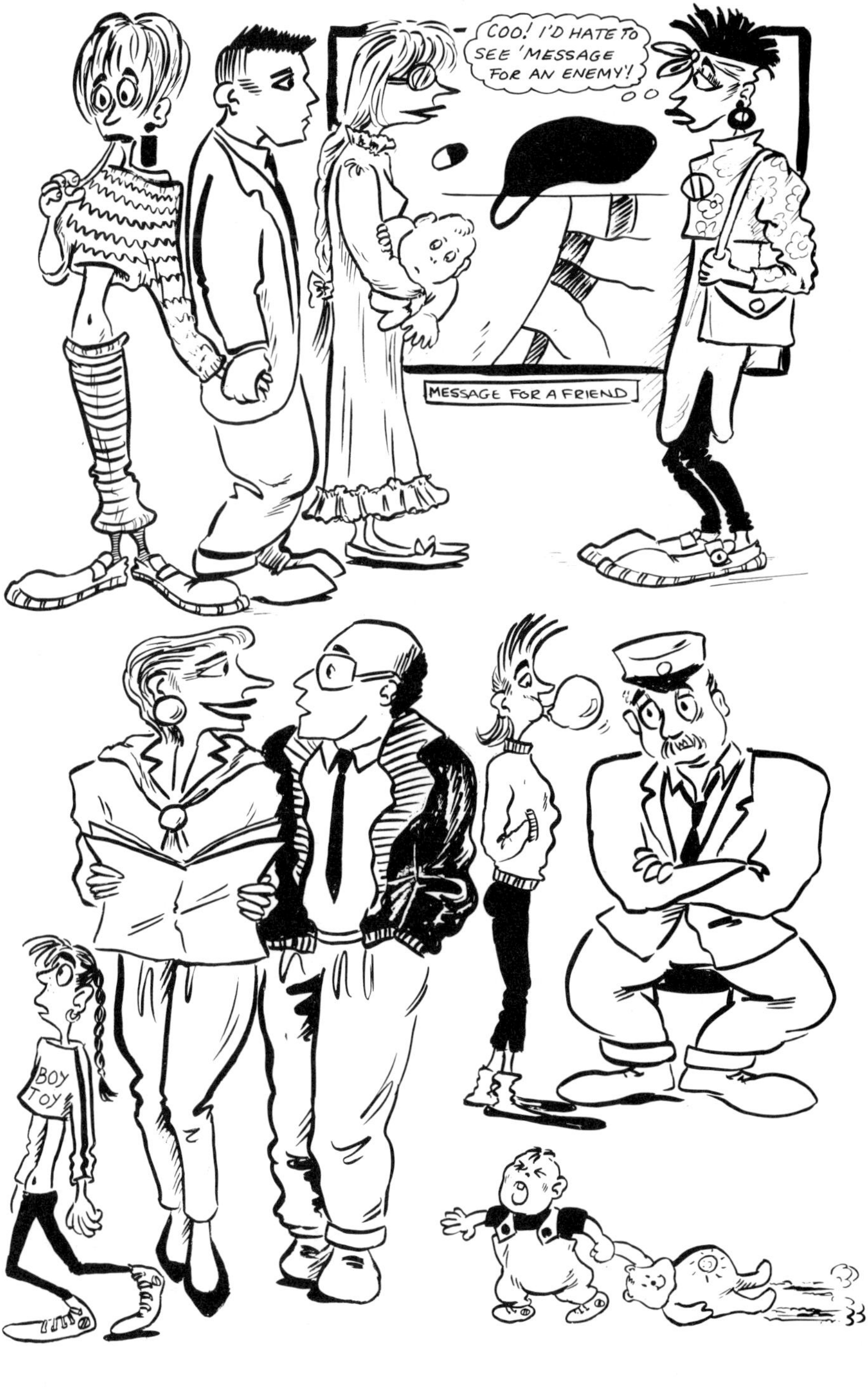

COO! I'D HATE TO SEE 'MESSAGE FOR AN ENEMY'!
MESSAGE FOR A FRIEND
BOY TOY